ACTION!

ACTION!

Memoirs of a Spectator

The Films of John Ford

J. M. Tasende

Ediciones Polígrafa

Photographic material courtesy of The Lilly Library, Indiana University,
Bloominton, Indiana, obtained through the genrous cooperation of Mr.
Dan Ford.

Cover photo *The Searchers*
Warner Bros. Studios

Design: Estudi Polígrafa / Salvador Bocharán
Colouproofs: Estudi Polígrafa / Borja Ardite
Coordination: Montse Holgado
Copy editing: Aitor Tasende
Printing and binding: Futurgràfic, Barcelona

ISBN: 978-84-343-1161-9
(ISBN-10: 84-343-1161-5)
Dep. legal: B 36.041 – 2007 (Printed in Spain)

ÍNDEX

*To Cain, anonymous mentor of
memorable cinematic experiences*

Reality is fluid and only remains in our imagination,
a journey through life taken with pain or joy;
everything else is almost always fantasy.

I have the feeling of being pushed to the center of a gigantic stage by those who wish to see me sing and dance to the beat of a rhythm I do not recognize. Without being able to avoid it, a stage fright takes hold of me and keeps me paralyzed in the center of the platform. I search for an exit, but all escapes have been carefully blocked by those who have come to entertain themselves at the anticipated clumsiness they predict in my movements. I try to disguise my inaptitude, just as the chords of a music I am unable to identify tentatively reach me, encouraging me to improvise a dance I have never rehearsed before. The exciting evocation of amusing experiences impels me to attempt a few moves in response to the sound, even though I am not able to figure out where it is coming from. Like an exhalation the resonance produced by strange instruments fills the entire auditorium, but mockingly appears to only be directed to me and I can't identify the tune. It is impossible to tell if it is a waltz or a rumba, a common tango or even a swing, nor does it appear to be a suggestive and erotic conga, or any other known rhythm. My hesitant steps are made even less sure when I suddenly recall the grotesque movements of drunken dancers I viewed in amazement for the first time a long time ago; like an indistinct whirlwind, distant journeys through sordid backrooms as a curious observer come to mind. I remember the first time I was in front of an audience as a professional athlete; an occasional airy presentation, certain small successes without any real relevance, and a long experience in failure. In contrast, on an imaginary screen the graceful silhouette of Fred Astaire appears. With unequalled dexterity, he shifts his fluid figure from one side to another of a very different and luxurious stage. With this double vision, I try to fight my insecurity and keep my footing on the platform. One must be optimistic: There might be someone tolerant enough and of a generous spirit, kindly willing to find some merit in the effort I am making. In any event, it is too late to go back. I'm also encouraged by the fact that results obtained by the more gifted usually only impress those who do not understand the significance of these achievements. Let's take heart and continue. According to these experts, nobody has a second chance to make a good first impression, so failure cannot befall us twice for the first time. One could add that success has a better chance of catching up to us if we don't strain to run in front of it too much. Inspired by the certainty of these discoveries, I will dare to begin the first steps of this undefined dance. I will try not to take myself as seriously as those already rewarded by fame; I am going to endeavor to be less solemn than those who enjoy the fruits of celebrity.

I'm not offended by the laughter of the few spectators who have come to see me stumble–amusedly witnessing the failed efforts I am making to dance, while commenting sarcastically upon the clumsy and stuttering attempt to follow the music. I am even less concerned that anyone attending this rehearsal out of curiosity might accuse me of getting the verses wrong. Besides, I have never been completely satisfied with my results obtained in the past, and the considerable risk that some of you will disagree with my commentaries did not alter my determination to get these pages printed. I am used to this, and it doesn't bother me as long as what I am saying is understood. Even so, there are two things in particular that I find alarming: To be boring, or misinterpreted because I am not able to explain myself well enough. I want to be sure this is not the case, without worrying too much about being accepted or rejected, though it doesn't mean I do not appreciate the opinion of others. This preoccupation probably leads me to reiterate and not care about any particular literary style. I don't know if I have anything worthy to say. Just like a young Hamlet, I, too, have my doubts whether to face, or not, life's challenges–even if on a smaller scale. One of these disturbing challenges might be finding out if the lyrics of the song that I am trying to follow lack merit, are simply absurd, or if the rhythm that accompanies them at least belongs to a particular musical school. It is difficult for the paternal specter to whisper the answer in my ears or carve its response on the wall.

Like my improvised dance, the lack of definition in the music, and the indistinct prose, these pages escape from my hands on their way to the printer without anyone being able to classify them within a recognizable philosophical tendency. It can only be identified by what the text does not encompass: It is not a proper chronicle, nor can it be classified within the biography genre without violating the fundamental principles of this literary specialty. No one with any knowledge could say that it is a cinematic critique. It does not have the appearance of a novel at all, although it could be one if a detailed outline of its gestation were done. From the beginning, my story doesn't really follow the norms of fiction. Even so, not even the most optimistic of readers can be certain that the author is attempting to duplicate reality. It is not a collection of historic data (my limited knowledge prevents this), and it would be dishonest to represent it as some sort of comedy, even as a pretext to hide my ignorance, though often done by snobs. Such a farce, in addition to being unjust and offensive to you, would also be an unbearable torture for me. It might only be a game or a pretext I have found to transmit certain ideas in my head–that which the Italians usually call a *divertimento*. Ideally, I would prefer it to be a tribute to the one who knew how to inspire the desire to delve into the depths of the human heart, and a diatribe against those who throughout life have sown our path with falsehoods. But, aside from my wishes, I fear this text might only turn out an extensive, albeit incomplete, cryptogram that the reader can interpret in whatever manner preferred, as all answers–whatever they might be–are correct. In spite of the subject's uncertainty and its risky setting, I have decided to put my optimism to the test by cautiously advancing into a territory full of surprises; sometimes I try to steady my unsure footing in the fog. I have come to realize that tackling a subject that can't even be precisely defined is a bit worrisome for a novice explorer like me. It is particularly overwhelming to recognize the unpredictability and difficulty of the journey that awaits us. I know I am trying to approach another's thoughts, and to do this I am relying only on the cinema as a stage and as a silent emcee, the master that has inspired my daring monologue. Timidly I began this exciting excursion in pursuit of the trail left by a passionate genius, and now I find myself in a trance attempting risky pirouettes on an uneven and rough surface.

As we have already established, the observations that appear in this text do not constitute in any way a film critique–at least not in the sense to which the public is accustomed to receiving weekly cinematic evaluations. Any newspaper or television network would instantly fire a critic who tried to comment on a movie in the manner in which I do so here. These methods of information must respond to the expectations of an audience captivated by the images of the actors and actresses from the most recent movie they have seen. Within the established standards, the press must share the tastes of the majority of the people and identify itself with the cult of the stars, practiced by a large sector of the public. I don't find anything censurable in this; I for one am also capable of appreciating virtuosity. Even so, I don't know how to adapt my criteria to that of most critics. It is difficult for me to distinguish the qualities that the connoisseurs find in every gesture, and I resist contemplating cinema as a stage conceived only so that a series of more or less competent individuals display their acting abilities while being compensated with exorbitant sums of money. The retelling of their brilliant performances I leave to my nonexistent manicurist in the imaginary beauty salon that I have no intention of visiting. I agree with John Ford: The less actors act, the better. I am amused by those who have managed to develop their own personalities and consistently portray them in every movie they appear in, like Buster Keaton, Bela Lugosi, Marilyn Monroe, Charlie Chaplin, Cary Grant, Steve Martin, Boris Karloff, Katherine Turner, Lee Marvin, Peter Lorre, Mae West, or Barry Fitzgerald. I suspect that the character portrayed by W.C. Fields was not fictitious. The dramatic abilities of actors and actresses have never interested me. To me it is always the director who fails or achieves his aim. As far as everything else is concerned, I will limit myself to offering a single suggestion to those interested in approaching this passionate subject: All the experts, including the most demanding of critics, should recognize that even the most gifted of actors has been unable to surpass the natural acting ability of Lassie in each of her appearances.

Without attempting to be solemn, it is impossible for me to conceive of an art form reduced to the superficiality of a competition between comedians, to be celebrated by those who confuse trivia with culture. The massive amount of information to which we are subjected does not contribute in any way to establish the differences between concepts, nor does it contribute to clarify in the least the profound importance that culture should have within or outside film. Even though knowledge has been extended to a larger public, it has not helped at all in establishing common norms of analysis or even in bettering the quality of communication between us. Even so, without guaranteeing any positive result, I promise to try. I will begin by saying that in art, I am not interested at all in the accessorial, just as in architecture I am irritated by that which strives to be noticed. There is also no merit in repeating that which someone has already said better and with more impact, even if it were by different methods. I suppose that comments like these will not satisfy the traditionalist who believes that there is no room for personal initiative in conception of a film, that cinema should be the loyal instrument of literature or limited to chronicling history. Whoever considers this to be the case, and believes that cinematography is obligated to follow the course traced by any other cultural manifestation, is wrong. Those who read me must not think that this dissertation has the intention of being deep. But neither does it fit the criteria of those who view cinema as a casual entertainment similar to that witnessed in a routine conversation on the weather or of a ball game.

Having said this, to avoid disappointing anyone, you must give up the hope of being in agreement with me very often and, finally, don't look for information here that can be easily found anywhere else!

The speculations that follow are only an experiment, and I am not sure of its nature. Let's try to invent a name for it that might restore my battered vanity and at the same time reassure whatever conscience, currently in danger of excommunication, I might still have. Even so, for those in search of a spiritual guide, it is time to throw this book to the voracity of the flames. Those who do not have a fireplace at their disposal are at liberty to look away and seek refuge in the farthest part of the planet, where some persistent stranger determined in imposing his presence will not be able to reach you to recite this dissertation. Let's suppose that the reduced number of people that are witnessing this hesitant and tentative kinetic/musical/literary experiment are tolerant enough, and let's give these unsure leaps an ambitious classification that will encourage our spirits as well as provide those who feel curiosity about the chosen subject a warning beforehand of the sinister proposals of the author. I must admit that the designation of this irreverent experiment is capriciously ambiguous and has not been selected to give any indication as to any significance the text might have. With the same unjustified criteria it could have been given other much more impressive titles: *The Future Testament*, *Faust in Paradise*, or *The Damn Comedy*, which would have been equally useless in figuring out the content of the book without paging through it. I will respond to the curiosity of the half dozen persons who, with certain irony, have asked what I have been writing about. But first let us follow protocol and drift off course to the day of the unveiling of the plaque commemorating the one thousandth performance, as they do in theater, before characterizing the contents of the book. Once we have done this, let us define it with the descriptive "auto-reflexography," promising for the tranquility of the determined reader that this word will not be repeated again. We shall see if this far-fetched term–softening the fears that afflict me–has the virtue of encouraging the audience; let us see if this gives some security to my steps. Perhaps this way, my two left feet will be able to glide more gracefully across the surface of the extensive stage.

* * *

Some time ago my wife, Helen, asked me to write down some of my experiences for our children. Something nearly impossible for me: Being a man of action, it is very difficult for me to talk about what I do. There are also a couple of other powerful reasons to discourage this. She might be wrong about the effect this could cause in the family, and I doubt that there are more than a dozen persons who might be interested in what I might have done during the course of my life. Besides, the journeys of people through different scenarios sound better when told by others, whatever their intentions might be. Those who practice this narrative specialty naturally favor analyzing their victims or heroes according to their own particular preferences. Even so, they must adjust their criteria to certain restrictions. The lives of exceptional beings or persons who have distinguished themselves in a certain specific activity immediately present two possibilities: Submission to the objective criticism of those affected by their actions or leave the story of their deeds to the virtuosity of the pen inspired to project the image of the subject for posterity. There is no cause for alarm: At the moment neither Plutarch nor Stendhal are available, and if they were, I doubt they would be very interested in me or in chronicling events with no historical relevance. It is also necessary to note that I have never been distinguished in the way that perhaps Truman Capote, or at least me, would have liked. Oh well, I must resign myself and do what I can, the best I can. Even so, as I am even more bewildered when speaking about myself, everything that refers to me personally must fit in three or four pages at the most. Nonetheless, I think I must give warning before continuing: The lack of proper sentence structure has been classified–perhaps by Cervantes–as "Biscayne syntax." This isn't a coincidence, as I am a native of Bizkaia. But I also have a good excuse for destroying two languages: Recently it seems as though everyone is writing books, so why shouldn't I?

A strange sensation of guilt invades me, and there is something I have managed to discover about myself while saturating each page with words. The effort I have to make to write properly is depressing, but this discouraging feeling hasn't impeded me from continuing this experiment, because, apparently without knowing it, I am a bit of a masochist. My daughter Betina emphatically disputes this supposition. She feels it is a sadistic instinct, concealed until now, that leads me to interrupt important chores at any hour of the day to bring her attention to improvised paragraphs. Thanks to her extraordinary and–in spite of what she says–voluntary, collaboration, I have been able to give some coherence to my writings. Between the two of us we have finished this dissertation done almost simultaneously in two languages. I am not a writer; this and other limitations of mine have made her work that much harder, but loaded with patience, she has been correcting some of the defects that filled my dissertation. I must recognize that only with her support have I felt capable of carrying out this effort. The ideas are mine; the writing, both in English and Spanish, is hers. There are others who have influenced this improvised experiment in great measure: Helen never makes demands and asks for little. I have never denied her anything in the past and now is not the time to start. With her discreet style, Mary Beth Hynes Petersen, collaborator and friend of more than twenty-eight years, subtly gave direction and encouraged me to put my thoughts in writing and, afterwards (every time she had a chance), made appropriate corrections to the text. The irritation that mistakes produce in my son Aitor, and which he has never stopped showing, changed my habits from the very first time we looked each other in the eyes and now with obstinate insistence demands unattainable perfection from this essay. His frustration will be inevitable. Even so, he has made the final corrections without protest. Among those who have helped with certain chapters of this experiment, Professor Tom MacCary has contributed with his expert advice, pointing out mistakes and giving these pages more of an English undertone. With kind disposition, Patricia Amaya and Paz Bilbao have both proofread my numerous grammatical errors in order to try to make the Spanish version as correct as possible. The generous sense of my friend David Finn–Florentine from 57th Street and an enthusiastic promoter of culture–made this publication possible, and his recommendations have been very valuable in the necessary lengthening of this risky and perhaps somewhat capricious dissertation. Thanks to my family and friends, this exhibition of thoughts that originated in my adolescence, and which I am trying to recount today, has resulted less rambling and disorderly than it would have had I not been able to count on their help and advice.

Don't expect great revelations, significant opinions, or even minor gossip; just a small, unfinished book. I lack the ability to refer to anecdotes. Events remain in my mind only due to their significance and disappear if they do not respond to a particular reason. This mental characteristic requires that I constantly ask myself why, and even though I try to conduct myself in a rational manner, I do so only out of habit, without any particular method. I cannot concentrate on something for very long. I must immediately go to the inside of a gift without even noticing the outwardly appearance. At the same time, my offering never impresses with its countenance, which is often battered. There is nothing I can do to make the packaging appear acceptable. Just as the wrapping I give it will never reach its destination in good shape, the clarity I strive to give these ideas I am unable to adorn with an eloquence that might make them appear more seductive or at least appear better-presented. Form is definitely not my strength. We shall see if at least this time we find something of value in the depth of the subject matter. From this point on I will endeavor to write only about what I think, based only on what I have read or seen, not what I do or have tried to do in the past. What I put to the consideration of the reader is the evidence of a criterion that has been forged through film and literature. Let's see if there is anything of substance here.

The determination to fill these pages was done with many reservations: I have lived intensely without taking time to make detailed notes, nor have I ever had the disposition necessary for accumulating data. Therefore, many of the more substantive experiences will undoubtedly be left out of any biographical attempt. On the other hand, my journey through this world has been fairly amusing; those who usually chronicle their own lives are often individuals who have generally led a sedentary and fairly boring existence. I am certain this isn't my case, which is why this attempt is in essence the recapitulation of a life, carried out through reflections rather than memories. I am not setting out–nor is it within my reach–to create a literary feat. I must reconcile myself with reciting the words of the song that I like, and dancing to the rhythm of the music that I have heard someplace before. In spite of all this, and in order to give a certain weight or at least some coherence to this commentary, I think I should write a few lines to establish who I am and the origin of my thoughts, which–in spite of what you might think–is modest and not very ambitious; achieving concise thoughts pretty much covers my intellectual aspirations. Searching for truth, I defend the right to make mistakes in my opinions. I believe in free analysis and I appreciate the correction of my blunders, but I do not accept being prohibited from making those mistakes. Those who do not tolerate errors in others end up condemning right answers. They have the same inclinations of an inquisitor, the soul of a bureaucrat, and the mentality of a cleric.

I must now apologize for not having been able to satisfy the wishes of those who insisted that I should make a more extensive and detailed reference to some of the activities that I have been involved in during the past years. I must also apologize for not having mentioned certain episodes of my life that some naïve admirer might have considered memorable. To narrate my own experiences would take more time than I have available, and I also don't think I am suited to do this. I am not interested in the idea of bringing up the past, or in hiding it, and I think that autobiographies usually seem to be only a form of auto-representation, written almost always with the intention of hiding rather than revealing something. Of course there are exceptions: Giacomo Casanova, apparently a fairly sedentary man with an enviable imagination, almost solemnly transmits his sensual fantasies. Conversely, Henry Fielding, a contemporary of his, writes a book of fiction with great humor in which he is actually present in several of the events he relates and might even have been the main protagonist. In spite of the disparity in literature and personalities, both of them were founders of a school destined to be followed by the celebrities of the moment, actors in decline, and retired basketball players. Then came the Marquis de Sade, an anticlerical moralist inspired by the depraved behavior of certain members of the clergy who dedicated his literary talent to discrediting them. It isn't difficult to imagine a diligent cleric in Charenton, converting the manuscript of what would have been another denigrating text by the French scholar against the church into the "memoirs" of the Marquis. In addition to scandalizing puritan gentlemen and stimulating the imagination of hysterical ladies while contributing with his name to the enrichment of the vocabulary of all languages, with little or no thanks, this persecuted noble Frenchman was a sex explorer who preceded the salacious erotic hypotheses of Sigmund Freud, and did so with ingenuity. But returning to the subject, the self-representation as far as I am concerned has at least one inconvenience: To represent yourself you have to be a little bit of an actor and, although a well-known authority once said "all the world is a stage," I do not have the most minimal histrionic vocation.

J.M.T.

KENNY BELL

The old house of Aitor's* children,
charred and devastated
by the furious cruelty of his enemies.
The episode that Walt Whitman,
from his majestic beard,
was unable to describe,
and the incisive eye of John Ford,
through his Irish nostalgia,
predicted without knowing.
The mournful song Dixie might have sung.
The Diaspora of the defeated.
What she suffered,
and what I have felt.
Ancient American tale with no ending.

These fourteen lines are an oration with which I feel the need to begin this monologue. A pagan prayer dedicated to my mother, who continues to be my inspiration and guide. In my mind as a child, only what she sowed was able to grow and with time give some meager fruit. Her hand led me for the first time to the movies and to school, precisely in that order.

Beyond the vagaries of destiny, to the sound of the sirens warning of the threat of bombs, from within my mother's arms I would contemplate the smiling white face of the moon, with the eyes and mouth of an enchanting woman. Taking refuge, lying in the tunnel like railroad ties, we waited for danger to pass. Later on, vengeance and hate would come from outside the country, and because of it, peace became more ominous than war.

Years later, while still a child, every day upon entering the school all students had to pray and intone several patriotic hymns prior to going into our respective classrooms. Once inside, new chants and prayers could be heard from each room, enlivening the hallways with their interminable repertory. Once this was over, classes could begin. Before leaving the campus, there would be more prayers and singing. It might be hard to believe that, in spite of so much animation, our

---

* Character from Basque mythology, possibly related to the Scandinavian Thor.

childhood was so sad. Giuseppe Tornatore would understand what I am talking about. This onslaught did not have the expected results, but did leave me with a habit I try in vain to correct: I'm inclined to recite my convictions out loud, which leads some to believe that I am speaking directly to them. From that limited education and profuse indoctrination, all that remains in me are insignificant vestiges of a questionable culture. On the other hand, without even trying, film had an enormous effect in my initial formation and later established my fondness towards books. Little by little, film generated doubts about the didactic intentions forced upon us by our dogmatic mentors, and I eventually broke away. With the help of literature, I began to question all teachings directed at reducing the freedom to choose, and later on I became accustomed to thinking for myself. The frustrated result of that educative effort is an irreverent and agnostic being who scorned the nationalism they attempted to impose on him.

In the footprints of the past,
there are traces of the future.

At the end of the war in Europe, my mother began preparations for our escape from that miserable panorama offered to us by the future of our country. This decision, the same as the most insignificant act of her life, was always directed towards finding some benefit for my future. That courageous woman dedicated her existence to preventing, as much as possible, those life shaking and distressing experiences from reaching me. That is what she did at the beginning of that voyage, hiding the negative aspects of our uprooting. What to my childlike fantasy was an exciting adventure signified a painful exile for her. Of that dramatic departure from the port of Santurtzi, I only recall a vague memory of aunts and cousins that came to see us off without knowing when we would see each other again. My thoughts were occupied imagining the emotions that awaited us and planning the journey that we would make through countries I only knew from the movies. The political circumstances of the moment forced us to pass through the United States before arriving in Mexico, and on the morning of Thanksgiving Day 1946, we stepped onto a dock at the port of the island of Manhattan. New York responded perfectly to my expectations and the image that I had of that city from the silver screen. The course we followed on a Greyhound bus to the frontier also gave me a sensation of passing through a country I already knew. In contrast, our encounter with Mexico gave the impression of having landed on an unknown planet. Nothing the Mexican cinema had shown me corresponded with the reality we were witnessing. Finally, we crossed the Sierra Madre during a memorable odyssey, in the company of chickens and pigs on board a Mexican bus, preceding Walter and John Huston filming their unforgettable movie. I must say we did not find any treasure either.

During my adolescence, which takes place in Guadalajara and Mexico City, sheltered by the smiling abnegation of my mother, I went to the movies with unusual regularity. At the beginning I made a point of attending the first showing of each movie. Later on, almost every afternoon I would watch at least a couple of them and after that, in the Mexican capital, I would occasionally manage to watch seven films in a single day. My fondness for the cinema was becoming obsessive, developing into a habit that continued through a period of dissipation and thoughtlessness of my youth. At the end of my adolescence I was able to find a nocturnal occupation that facilitated my movie attendance even more. Soon afterwards, as a professional athlete, I had time to go to the movies, get drunk, and experiment romantically with the opposite sex. For a few years, that comprised my two other favorite occupations. At that point I couldn't think of anything else that was worth the free time left over from playing Jai-Alai. I retired a long time ago from that profession. Today I go to the movies infrequently, and I've slowly stopped drinking alcohol. During that period of my life I discovered an excellent Cuban magazine, and in it were movie reviews by Cain, who in my judgment is the most lucid writer ever concerned with cinema besides Umberto Eco. Thanks to this writer, I realized that I was not hallucinating. I wasn't the only one to see assorted and profound values below the surface of the cinematic narrative. Before Kurosawa gave us his prodigious lesson, we had discovered that film was not a simple successive reproduction of images. It was also a subjective approach the twentieth century had provided the mind to more deeply observe life. Subsequent fortuitous events oriented my activities in a direction even I had not imagined. By some whim of fate, from night to day I found myself converted into an art dealer, and due to the demands of my new occupation some of my habits changed. As a result of the obligations imposed by my new profession, my visits to the movie theaters became less frequent until they were sporadic at best. In spite of no longer being a diligent viewer of every new release, my reflective disposition with regards to the cinema continued unchanged. The subsequent professional relationships that I established with artists of other disciplines, I believe, has allowed me to make instructive comparisons of the significance of film in relation to other expressions of the arts.

* * *

For the greater part of the past century, film has been the most important instrument of education for millions of people. Seeking only temporary amusement, our generation was also taught by this marvel of modern technology that allowed us to dream. Our generation witnessed how this casual entertainment was gradually accepted as a new art form and eventually, for many, became the most important artistic breakthrough of our time. Cinema has been many things. In some countries, it was the defense that helped children and young people resist the indoctrination unleashed by a variety of dogmas, an experience that encouraged reasoning in the face of those doctrines. In such times, disoriented by propaganda, we saw human nature in all its greatness and misery through film. The episodes transmitted to us on the silver screen seemed more real than the news reports doled out by the government, and conditioned us to reject the images offered to us by sects. Film also spoke to us about a better life, with greater opportunities and the possibility for each of us to forge our own destiny. For the young, it was like an open window to a promising future with greater freedom. In certain latitudes, where the alternatives were limited and actions so restricted, movies represented the only approach that would allow freely analyzing and choosing one's ethical values, encouraging the young to continue in their quest. These were times of war, and the Allied triumphs in the battlefields were in our eyes the defeat of oppression and censure. The American Dream paraded through films like a rainbow after the storm; it was the beacon that showed us what could be beyond the nightmare that smothered our lives.

For me it had an even deeper significance: It filled those moments of desolation in my childhood with promising images, and, as I matured, it became an occasion for reflection and hope. During those years in the Basque Country, the fanatical and ecclesiastical censorship, obsessed with sex, was also part of a ferocious political persecution. At our age–even though we had no other experience–we recognized the effects of censure, exerted by the obtuse troglodytes who persisted in indoctrinating us. We tried to find hidden meanings in the scenes shown in the theater and to decipher cryptic messages in the movies–almost all of them American–which, in those times, came to us after considerable delay. It was a sort of amusing game, trying to imagine the passages of the film that had been removed due to censure. We became impassioned in our search to find some detail that might have escaped the film vandals. It is understood that an absolutely indispensable condition to being a censor is an utter lack of any sensibility whatsoever, and during the course of the movie, we would find something that the agents in charge of our thinking had been incapable of conceiving. Our enthusiasm was such that at times it appeared there was some sort of code by which we were in communication with the authors that was not apparent to the ever-vigilant censors.

* * *

The influences that we experience over time sometimes translates into impulses that–though their significance is unrecognized–encourages us to proceed through life, at times in search of an ideal, at others running after an illusion. Those close to us influence our behavior, while others, without knowing us, nevertheless prompt the paths of our lives to take unexpected courses. Only a few privileged minds have the power to significantly influence vast numbers of people and, on occasion, humanity in its entirety. We qualify these individuals as heroes, leaders, artists, or geniuses. The impact John Ford's work has had in our time has transcended its cinematographic sphere and–even when it might have held a different significance for each of us–changed the way many of us observe our surroundings. I can say that his films have most influenced my view of movies and even of art in general. He is to me, and many others, a hero of the twentieth century.

Recognition of his tremendous contribution inevitably leads me to recall the past; otherwise it wouldn't be possible for me to pay homage to this extraordinary creator. I must admit that when I analyze his work, I cannot find a way to separate it from certain episodes of my life. I will follow this course–somewhat more personal and perhaps a bit disorderly–hoping that, in spite of this, I will be able to make my observations comprehensible and perhaps even give them some coherence. I don't aspire to make any discoveries, only to spontaneously reflect on known facts. I do not expect to effect an exhaustive examination of his personality, nor do I have the intention of compiling a complete analysis of the work of this prolific director. To do so, the publication of several volumes, not to mention knowledge greater than what I possess, would be necessary. The following commentaries will be more of a confession of the effects the films of John Ford have had on me. I understand that these conclusions must be subjective and, consequently, open to debate; only that which is transcendental requires no criticism. I also think that without undertaking all of the subjects he touched, it is still possible to sketch a defining pattern by analyzing his work in general. Since he tried to transmit his thoughts to us through movies, I believe that through his films, we can come to understand his purposes in some measure. After all, he, too, tried to understand us from the other side of the camera. Either way, there was always something he wanted to tell us about ourselves and about him. Even when the incisive and seductive discourse of John Martin Feeney or Sean Aloysius O'Feeney–John Ford–shining like a revelation, comes close to my image of the complete and perfect artist, I shall try to remain objective.

If I extend myself too much in these personal ramblings, it is only with the intention of explaining that my point of view originates from a fresh perspective. It does not come from the mind of a person connected to the film industry, nor is it the consequence of a meticulous study of film. What I want to point out is that my examination of this director and his films is more emotional and biological rather than historical or technical, and although it might not have any other value, it at least has the intention of being original. I plainly believe that to describe the origin of these ideas–by explaining a little bit about myself–they might become more intelligible for the reader, and perhaps then my observations will deserve to be judged with a wider criteria and greater benevolence.

Life invites us to action;
we will do so with passion or indifference.

It remains to be seen what educational value film has had for nearly an entire century now, but the overseers of the first generation held it in very little esteem. Priests as well as teachers tried to keep us away from the movies. They considered cinema an impediment to learning and an obstacle to acquiring any real culture. I don't know if it had the same significance for others, but as far as I was concerned, movies were a happy awakening and an exercise in imagination. Later they became a habit that helped me reflect. Taking into consideration my experience, I've concluded that perhaps the academics of our time concentrated too much on the accumulation of information, neglecting the exercise of the mind and the development of understanding. Those of us who believe this think that, perhaps in the future, film and television might complement the formal education given today by academic institutions. Whatever its future, from the very start film was a refuge for those of us who saw school as a cloister of arbitrary discipline, or, sometimes, a nest of doctrinal intolerance.

My cinematic experiences were happy from the start. I saw my first movie with my mother. It was a short feature film by Mack Sennett that left in me an indelible memory of automobiles colliding and individuals running in all directions. I couldn't have been more than three years old and the impression those scenes made in me still remains. Charlie Chaplin, Buster Keaton, and Joe Brown were my first heroes of the silver screen. I was spared the melodrama of Valentino and company, for reasons as unknown as they are fortuitous. Later on, out of curiosity, I watched some of those films and they, too, made me laugh. I think that back then, children comprised a proportionally larger part of the movie-viewing public; perhaps that is one of the reasons why cinema was rejected as a true art form for so long.

Stan Laurel and Oliver Hardy mark the beginning of sound motion pictures for me. I don't know why, but earlier movies with soundtracks barely caught my attention. Surprisingly, the repertory and resources of these two amazing comedians were–in spite of sound–more elemental and accessible than those of their predecessors in silent movies. The incidents and situations that would arise during the course of their films fascinated us children. We considered them our friends, with whom we had established a warm and loving relationship. Almost at that same time, W.C. Fields came on the scene, an actor born to play himself: A personality torn from the pages of a novel by Charles Dickens. It would have been unforgivable for George Cukor not to entrust him with the representation of Mr. Micawber in *David Copperfield*. But with the exception of a few noteworthy examples, in the beginning, films with soundtracks couldn't be compared to what up to then had been achieved by those masters of silent movies.

* * *

The ingenuity of the very first directors of silent films became apparent to me through their comedies–true masterpieces–made with extremely limited means. I became acquainted with the films of D.W. Griffith much later; even then, this director hinted at the tremendous prospects that were emerging in this new art as a fertile field of experimentation. *The Birth of a Nation* is the masterpiece that proves that the greatness of a film is not in the sound nor in the color, nor even in the special effects, but in the intensity and ability with which the director is capable of transmitting his ideas and feelings. Afterwards, with the advent of sound, Orson Welles would demonstrate the same thing through a much more intimate subject, *Citizen Kane*. I mention these examples not because I think they are the only movies that deserve commentary. I do so only with the object of illustrating my point of view and because each of these two films marks a very well-defined period in the history of cinema.

Griffith is a legitimate forerunner to the career of John Ford, and this link can help us understand his relationship with Hollywood. To better study the work of someone and to be able to grasp their intentions, it is necessary to have some knowledge of their background and the atmosphere in which they developed their work. I think that in the case of John Ford, prior to making reference to the depth and dimension of his work, it would be useful to reflect on the times in which he lived and to consider film in general. I must limit myself to only these two subjects since I am unfamiliar with the technical process of filmmaking, and have never delved into its inner workings. I know film as a spectator, someone who has watched it evolve technically and who has witnessed the parade of great films, some mediocre ones, and a few truly brilliant. So I will only address what I have learned as a part of the viewing public, as someone who knows a little about the history of film, its glories and tribulations.

Even though I was not able to finish a formal higher education, I did have access to certain aspects of culture that have helped me to better understand the essence of cinema. My intention is not to approach the subject too extensively, but I hope I don't do it superficially either. I think this is only possible by broaching a wide variety of subjects that at first glance could be considered unrelated to this purpose. I fear that my digressions might appear too capricious and even inappropriate, but I don't think there are many issues that can be excluded from an activity where so many disciplines come into play and that deal with all aspects of existence. I am going to justify the need for my detours based on the cultural, sociological, ethnical, and psychological factors that intervene–even though they often remain hidden–in the creative process and affect the subconscious of those who participate in it. At the start of this study, I felt the need to examine the elements that influence artistic production, or at least those within my reach, which might explain the nature of the product–in this case a story photographed in motion. I hope this is somewhere on the horizon of my experience and within my abilities. I am not erudite; I am only an observer with a bit of knowledge and some ability to reason. I will follow through with this experiment by assuming cinematography to be my alma mater and John Ford the imminent master of that illustrious university.

Time is the other name
Man has given life; or death.

By chance, while watching the big screen that always offered some exciting
surprise, the passionate world of John Ford reaches me when I am still a child, but
already a veteran viewer of all kinds of movies (erudite in the limited trivia of
silent films). I knew the names of those featured in the talkies but ignored who
directed them. Then and for many years after, there was no reason for the spectator
to know the name of the director of the movie being shown, and no one bothered
to inform the public. It was much as it is today: A world of stars and big studios,
but apart from the silent comedies, the directors were unknown. Even then, the
acting qualities of the actors and actresses were publicly analyzed, along with
abundant information on their whims and flirtations. Even so, after silent movies,
while the public worship of film stars was heightened, we still did not know the
names of the authentic creators of the films. Recognition of the merits of the
author of a film is something the public has engaged in during the latter part of
the last century. This oversight of those truly responsible for the work, while
favoring the mundane, has gradually been corrected without the stars losing any of
their shine. The three "talkies"–*Mary of Scotland*, *The Informer*, and *How Green
Was My Valley*–that I considered my favorites belonged to the same director,
unknown to me. Television had not developed yet. Printed reviews of films barely
existed and abundant monographic publications were a thing of the future. Given
the circumstances, my first opinions of the performances were necessarily
autodidactic. These conclusions grew and intensified over time, but nothing has
occurred since then to change them. I made the connection between John Ford and
his films years later, during my adolescence, most of which took place in Mexico.
From then on it was easy for me to follow the course of his prodigious career.

My knowledge of the biography of John Ford comes through episodes of his life
that have been made public, the fragmented accounts that his friends have shared
with us and, of course, through repeated viewing of his films. The commentaries
that I have read about him have left me the impression of only scratching the
surface of his personality. Only recently have I had the opportunity to obtain two
excellent biographies, solidly documented, that include a complete chronology of

the life and work of John Ford. Perhaps the most insightful observation made on his abilities was that Ford was capable of seeing better with one eye than the rest of us can with two. I haven't had much luck with the interviews either. I've been unable to find out if someone ever asked him any interesting questions. His exasperation during the course of those dialogues does not surprise me. It is in his work where he responds with vigor, conviction, and tenderness to the incisive questions that he personally formulates; that and a large pile of photographs that captures the environment of a man of action, of profound and luminous thinking.

* * *

Emerging from silent film, John Ford was able to grasp the significance of the innovation of sound as no one else could. To him it was like a miracle he had been awaiting for many years. From everything that we can now theorize on this subject, Ford was intuitively able to clearly discern from his very first contact with sound in film. He understood that as a contrast, sound produced a new effect in silence, which was no longer a limitation and instead became a resource. With the introduction of sound, silence automatically becomes a new medium to reach the subconscious of the viewer, which Ford used to give greater eloquence to his images. With keen perceptiveness, he would find in the pauses that follow his laconic dialogues the emotional resources that helped stimulate the imagination of the public. Following a vague but suggestive phrase, an object, scenery, or sometimes the back of one of the characters projected against the light brings us all of the intensity of a scene. Ford used sound and silence to enhance or complement the dramatic impression of his photographic effects as no one had until then. Possessed with incredible talent, he placed emotions at the reach of anyone with a minimum of sensibility, and in doing so opened up an almost unlimited horizon of possibilities in cinema.

In the photographic frames of Ford–truly masterful works of composition–the intention of intensifying the emotion of each scene is very clear. The characters appear perfectly outlined on a well-defined background, both in the interior shots as well as when he filmed in open spaces. The camera is always precisely positioned at the desired level to obtain the necessary effect. Sometimes it contributes to the dramatic effect, while on other occasions he deliberately raises it in order to avoid melodrama. Everything is calculated for the purpose of creating a new reality, not with the intention of representing an event. The function of his photography is to give a sense of realism, more intense and credible than reality itself. This could appear to be a paradox but it isn't because Ford, a historian by vocation, only makes use of the subject matter of the chronicle. His objective is not to photograph history but to create the ambiance in which it develops. Those who try to reproduce a reality based on historical premises– which are almost always false–are presenting us with situations that fluctuate between the improbable and the impossible. Anyone who has seen the dramatized biographies on television or viewed historical films in Spanish will know what I mean. In contrast to this fake way of staging life by solemnly portraying trivialities on an artificial platform, he first creates a realistic and plausible environment, and then he imagines a credible relationship between the profoundly human characters so that these beings can be represented by individuals who barely need make an effort to act.

* * *

In Ford's cinema, emotions are projected through images, while dialogues are used for little else than to give ambiance to a scene. At times, sequences appear to remain inconclusive, in expectation that we will complete them on our own. The moments of silence are generally more eloquent than the dialogue itself; occasionally Ford finds a phrase that is also suggestive, not for what it explains but for what it implies: "Mac, have you ever been in love?" "No, I've been a bartender all my life." This enigmatic dialogue helps us understand the value of his silences. When hearing this apparently insignificant verbal exchange without even the most minimal relationship to the plot, a strong emotional reaction takes place inside us. Something is being revealed, an emotion we believe we understand but don't feel capable of explaining. John Ford was clearly aware of the possibilities and the limitations of film. He knew there is a subjective value in each movie that is outside the control of the director. When the story reaches the subconscious of the viewer it takes on a life of its own, beyond the authority of the narrator. Ford, having as much respect for us as for the topics he worked with, lets us think and come to our own conclusions on what we are viewing. Afterward, in *Rashomon*, Akira Kurosawa would take this very subjective speculation to its absolute limit.

Few creators have put so much of themselves into their work. Through his films we can get to know John Ford almost as well as if we had been with him his whole existence. In his determination to produce a reality that was intense and almost tangible, Ford did not let the characters of the film escape their human condition, and he has the virtue of doing this while feeling compassion for their miseries and expressing reverent admiration of their dignity. The recurring landscapes in his films–even when they are frequent topics in his work–are treated with such delicacy and respect that they never appear as obsessions. Ireland is a frequent subject of his iconography, invariably reminiscent and suggestive. Ireland, dramatically glimpsed through the sea mist as it appears reflected in *The Informer* or the green and sweet Eire of *The Quiet Man*, are two very diverse American visions of his ancestral country. The scenery preferred by Ford–majestically visual–is Monument Valley. The open spaces of the American West are something of an extension of the sentimental and nostalgic Ireland of his ancestors. To him, there is an intimate relationship between these two distinctly different landscapes: Those who gallop through the plains and deserts of America are also Irish horsemen. In the course of his career, John Ford bequeathed us a vibrant testimony of American history as nobody in film has done to date.

Like William Shakespeare, John Ford also feels an intimate fascination for history, particularly our recent past–the time that has escaped through our hands. He has a sentimental passion to understand our predecessors. The narrative style of Ford–particularly during his last films–is as similar to Shakespeare as can be approximated in cinema. It is curious that he never tried to bring a work by the Bard to the silver screen, although recitals of passages from one of his tragedies or comedies are occasionally found in some of Ford's films. As in the work of this genial poet, all of John Ford's films are solidly documented, even when the subject might have been extracted from fiction and its relation with history is purely incidental. Ford prefers to follow the spirit of the story and its significance, rather than the elaborated text. He knows that history–as far as specifics–can be fantasy and whim in the best of cases and, in the worst, fallacy and vested lies. This can be verified with a little bit of experience: We all know that the official versions of some events are frequently less accurate than speculations. Ford tried to fill the existing void between historical fact and plausible circumstances in which a certain event might have taken place, and did so with imagination and grace, but also with honesty, without betraying history.

Ford is the inventor and conveyor of a language that has become the norm in cinematography. Thanks to him, the ethical and moral conflicts confronted by man have been presented to us through images that surpass the possibilities of theater and that the cinematographic community has accepted as the standard. Influenced by his inspiration, we have been viewers who have learned to observe the world assisted by a criterion that cinema has contributed to disseminate. Heartened by this certainty, I will make an attempt to penetrate the mind of the most prolific creator cinematography has had. The only means to figure out his personality that I have within reach is his work. This may be the riskiest of my convictions, but I believe that in some measure, the cinema is John Ford and John Ford is the cinema. After all, there are many other beliefs with less foundation than this that enjoy enormous prestige and even public acclaim.

John Ford belongs to the heroic generation of the past century. He knew how to assume this responsibility as a man and an artist and to reflect in his work the best of this romantic American pursuit. His movies are revolutionary in their focus as well as in their content. He directed the first feminist film, *Seven Women*. In *Sergeant Rutledge*, his camera approaches the racial theme in a rare context without superficially compassionate gestures or demagoguery. The behaviors of Fords characters contain a lot of him, of his illusions and his romantic and dignified approach to life. In his defense of John Mankevich, during the memorable meeting of the Screen Film Directors Association, in the face of the ominous omnipotence of Cecil B. de Mille, there is something of Ringo defending Dallas to the occupants of *Stagecoach*. The ambiance of camaraderie and loyalty that is implicit in his films is a reflection of the relationship he maintained throughout his life with his friends. That intense emotion that he manages to transmit through his movies is only possible if one believes in what is being said and if the ideas spontaneously spring from a generous and romantic spirit.

*Film is the only art where action and
images are captured in movement.*

The impression of movement through images was the idea behind the origin of the
cinema. Photography, the foundation upon which Impressionist painting evolved,
also gave rise to film. This new discovery becomes an art, influences one already
in progress, and spawns the cinematographer, who–along the way–becomes one
of the more creative instruments in the social revolution of the twentieth century.
The invention that Louis Jacques Daguerre placed at the disposal of the world
was destined to evolve in unsuspected directions and to enrich itself with audio
and visual effects that he never imagined. Each of the discoveries that are
combined with this technique of image reproduction opens a whole series of
possibilities for the artist. Sound, color, the application of special effects, and the
development of television each day offer the prospect of finding new ways to
reach the sensibility of the public. This process begins with the camera. From
then on, everything that surrounds man or that he is capable of creating is
condemned to being visually represented, and if so desired, this representation
acquires the ability of virtual movement.

Images in motion pursue a direction and through interrelated sequences suggest
events that comprise the narrative. To give coherence to the most elemental and
modest of cinematographic projects, the writer, whether part-time or professional,
is indispensable. Literature is the first thing that film is compelled to use. More
than anything else, literature will give the director the cinematic perspective that
will be so useful at the time of editing the movie. Indifferent to rank, film uses
great literature in the same manner as the most insignificant novel. The texts of
both will be liberally adapted to the movie by another specialized writer. Through
editing, a final self-critique will be carried out by the director of the film. The
narrative shown to us by the cineaste with the aid of pictures in motion is the
result of the imagination and ingenuity of generations, made possible by
twentieth-century technology. But to continue to grow, film has to return to the
past and refer to the rest of the arts. Of all the disciplines that have enriched
cinematography, only literature continues to be indispensable.

Literature is the fundamental means for the inception of any cinematographic work, but can frustrate those results if the director decides to sacrifice the development of the film out of loyalty to the literary text by rigorously adhering to it. This recurring mistake indicates a complete lack of knowledge of the essence of cinema. When the course of a novel is followed with excessive accuracy, the film will always flounder. For a movie to have impact and be able to penetrate, it is necessary for the story to be told according to the cinematic possibilities, not literary requirements. It does not matter how excellent the book or how deep its message. When it becomes a film it will only reflect the talent of the director. Neither film nor literature can imitate each other; in this sense they cancel each other out. However, film can definitely benefit from literature, although the latter does not have the ability to use film–at least it cannot do so to improve upon itself. On the other hand, a writer has certain advantages: All kinds of explanations can be given on the page of a novel, but if the movie director does this during filming, all is lost. The movie becomes a simple documentary of the book.

* * *

There always exists a technical factor that interferes with the most efficient transmission of an idea. In this manner, science, the great revolutionary, has influenced and transformed almost everything. Even when planet Earth was still in the dark, by exposing a venerable book to public opinion, the printer's press gave a devastating blow to the monopoly of the monasteries. Since then, those in power became vulnerable to the criticism of the writer, limitlessly repeated by the press. This machinery, conceived somewhere in a corner of Germany by Johann Gutenberg, finally put culture within the reach of many, brings about a rebirth throughout the continent for the thirst of knowledge and allowed Europe to scurry in search of its Greek origins. Henry Ford, with his technological concepts of industrialization as applied to consumption, unintentionally gave the progress of civilization a greater impulse than all of the social utopias put together. The founder of the Ford Motor Company, on his own and contrary to the rest of society, put in evidence what the world would verify in consternation almost a hundred years later: It is capital, not bureaucracy, that is the only "comrade" of labor. Hidden behind the prophet's beard of Karl Marx was the author of a farce. In spite of the invalidity of his social theories and the paralysis that his doctrines provoked in many creative minds, we can say that, even with those obstacles, science contributed to better our lives during the past century. Even so, it has not been able to determine the validity of art. The technique of transmitting moving images has revolutionized the panorama of visual arts during the twentieth century, even though as an essential part of the cinematic function, technology is far from a fundamental factor in elevating the quality of film–even while it consistently contributes to making it more spectacular and, consequently, more popular. The creative force continues to be in the human mind and will probably always be there. In film as in other disciplines, the work of art is insignificant or outstanding according to the ability of its creator. Technology can only contribute to facilitate the transmission of an idea, but not to conceive it. Prior to and after every technological innovation, numerous noxious movies have been produced, along with some prodigious masterpieces. Individuals without vocation or talent keep harvesting successes inside the film industry, while those more romantic and generous–following the path traced by John Ford–will continue to make it fertile and creative.

Even while science has been a great supporter of cinema and an indispensable element of its development, it cannot be said that film's artistic value is dependent on it. An avalanche of mediocrity has invariably followed all advancements in cinematographical technology. This is most likely for two reasons: The first is that not everyone is capable of adapting their abilities to the transition arising from changes in technology, particularly those movie directors who rely exclusively on their production knowledge. The other reason is that the public's curiosity for a new technique consigns to second place its interest in the quality of a film. In these circumstances, to achieve success the excellence of the product is no longer as essential as emphasizing the technical novelty to the public. Which is why during times of transition, the industry only incorporates that which has commercial possibilities, thereby giving entry to every incompetent individual unconcerned with the creative aspect of making a movie. The same thing that is happening now with special effects happened during the first few years of the advent of color and during the transition from silent to sound movies. It is much easier to use a technological achievement available to all than to create a work of art. The consequence is clear: While the public is enthused over the new invention, mediocrity takes over the field.

* * *

Sound, as an innovative resource, also brought with it a modification in the direction of ideas, requiring a different approach to the value of silence, and demanding a separate analysis on the psychological and emotional effects that this new cinema would exert on the public. Few directors and stars survived this spectacular technical advance; even Chaplin had serious difficulties in adapting to the latest technological procedure. This new method required a philosophical change in the relationship with the viewer and a different disposition towards the transmission of images. With the advent of sound, the movie director found that the actors' miming of emotions was no longer necessary and was considered ridiculous by the audience. Consequently, gestures no longer needed to be so pronounced and scenes had to be done with more subtlety. This entails a more delicate and precise editing process, if the intention is to better project the emotions felt by the characters. Once actors could speak on camera, their performances required less exertion and images acquired a more intimate dimension. It is discovered that in the dialogues, not only what is said but what is omitted has some value and the narrative could be presented more subjectively, giving spectators the opportunity to generate their own interpretation of the story. Even the concept of time underwent an appreciable change, acquiring new meaning. With time subordinated to sound and silence simultaneously, the psychology of the spectator is subjected to these two elements. Much later, in *Mr. Hulot's Holiday*, Jacques Tati would realize a brilliant attempt in this area. Sound is replaced by an almost telegraphic language of sequences and gestures, giving us the contradictory sensation of having watched an extraordinarily long movie that ended much too soon.

Just as shadows are perceptible only in contrast to light, the real emotional value of silence is perceived only upon the arrival of sound. Up to then, only action could be observed; silence had yet to be discovered. Prior to 1927 it would not have occurred to anyone to qualify a movie as silent. Sound was needed so that silence could be achieved in a film. By using sound only to give realism to a scene, John Ford was the first to discover the emotional wealth of silence, in contrast to music and synchronized dialogue. By intensifying the emotion of the moment through the gestures of the characters–with the aid of light and the photographic frame–sound became a part of the action and not just an explanation of what was happening onscreen. For the first time, the camera touched an emotional chord in the spectator, up to then unknown in film. John Ford used the advantage of sound with incomparable ability and rhythm, a style emulated by many later on.

With the arrival of sound, only the most creative directors realized what a brilliant future it would have in movie-making and that it wasn't only a technical advance to be commercially exploited. Apparently, the euphoria produced by this discovery continues. As it had to happen, when those interested in cinema exclusively as a revenue-generating industry were faced with this great innovation, confusion reigned in its every application that wasn't instantly profitable. Those who wanted to continue producing films of singular value had to struggle against the interests and incomprehension of the inept. Few were able to overcome this accumulation of circumstances, and a lot of time went by before film directors were able to make words reach the emotional value of action. Nunnally Johnson in *The Man in the Gray Flannel Suit* gives an eloquent demonstration of this possibility, constructing this film on a series of very effective dialogues and pauses charged with emotion. In many other films, the conversations of the characters only served to hide the inconsistencies of the movie. However, over the years, great films have been made thanks to the magic of sound. The list would be extensive before reaching *Traffic*, where Steven Soderbergh, in an original approach, introduces a solid colloquial language that leaves us trembling at its ominous drama. Sound liberated ideas, opened up possibilities, and stimulated the imagination of some, but also brought confusion and disorientation to others. It was necessary to confront the juncture and define the path to be followed. In the midst of this situation, the consequence of the disappearance of silent movies, John Ford arrives like a master tutor to give order to ideas, reason to the mind, and fire to our hearts.

* * *

When any mechanical advancement is used in mass production, it creates an immediate change inside society. But for this impetus to change artistic expression and gain validity, it is necessary to find the proper application for the new innovation and to know how to use it in art and not the other way around. When dialogues are finally synchronized with the vocal movements of the actors and other acoustic necessities of a movie, it was a notable cinematographic advancement, but it did not necessarily mean that the quality of a film had improved. Music also helped the development of the film industry, but until speech could be heard for the first time, its contribution was limited. Dialogues were able to give the cinematographic sense that had been missing, thus elevating music to an essential part of the movie. Music preceded the spoken word in film much as it did in the development of languages; however, over time language was the one that forced music to evolve. The same thing happened in film. Dialogue revolutionized the scene. Film only knows how to use both music and language without enriching them, but by circulating popular phrases and melodies, it has returned the favor, making these two cultural elements more popular.

The first musicals in black and white were only spectacular displays of stage design, much in the same manner of the current proliferation of "special effects." A further element was necessary prior to finding the formula that permitted the director to visualize a new style of film. With color it became possible to think about an original visual effect that would transform the expectations of the public and, when a viewer was so inclined, to also conceive of a production where the rules would change and the musical score could be glamorized. This also required greater imagination by the artist to take advantage of these innovations in benefit of art. A new system was created that was enthusiastically accepted by the spectator and, for more than a decade, the musical comedy dominated the cinematographic panorama. In this new cinema, through decoration, the splendor of the scenery and the enchanting music managed to immunize the public against their inclination towards more realistic movies. The director of musicals did not need to limit the narration to only those events essential to the story and could now freely extend themselves in trivial digressions without worrying about giving the film an unexpected outcome or trying to obtain the realism that the viewer used to expect in a movie.

* * *

The realism of the cinematic language must overcome everyday reality. What happens in a movie must obey a certain logic, not the whim of the movie director. The actors say what the director tells them to by way of a script and they move as he decrees, but the impression of being simple puppets must be dispelled when they appear on screen. The public needs to feel that these characters have lives of their own and that it is the circumstances determining all that occurs during the film. Everyday events with no particular meaning have no reason to be on the screen. Within the silver screen, everything must have a plausible explanation. Anachronisms and contradictions in narration are unacceptable in film. Absurdities transform drama into a mendacious farce and are only permissible in a comedy, and then solely when the story and the characters commit them deliberately, not at the capricious whim of the director. Harold Lloyd, the Marx Brothers, and Mel Brooks are the most conspicuous representatives of this school of nonsensical irreverence. Whoever makes the movie can give in to excess, but exaggeration must respond to an expressionist need. The subconscious of the viewer makes a quick distinction between excess and nonsense. If what is being narrated does not have a rational explanation, it will not give the sensation of reality necessary to reach the audience, and the story will not engage the public's sensibility.

Film is a contraction of space and, above all, economy in terms of time. A story or an event that occurs during the course of an entire day, month, year, must be summarized on the screen in about one hundred minutes. It must encompass only that which is relevant to making the narration understandable and reaching the heart of the audience. Within this code there is a variable that takes place prior to the onset of modern cinema and which develops after the arrival of television. The old silent comedies, as well as in television sitcoms currently being created for a more distracted and multi-tasking consumer, are made up of sequences where time does not exist outside of what we are watching. What we watch in half an hour is assumed to take place in thirty minutes. This is a different language that cannot be adapted to a movie plot with continuity; beginning, middle, and ending. Otherwise, the time in which a movie runs would be insufficient to cover the accumulation of trivial events that can happen during even five minutes' time to the characters in the cast. To project a few instances of the life of each would take months. If the intention is to synthesize an indeterminate length of time to less than two hours of film, it is necessary to establish an agreement between the director and the public: What is going to remain in the narration of the movie and what must be removed.

The restrictions that time imposes on cinematography have prompted some directors to defy this limitation. For nearly ninety minutes, the camera portrays the final seconds of life in the mind of the main character in the movie *American Beauty*. Of course, this symbolism is a game in which, with great talent, Sam Mendes tries to invert the relationship that film has had with time. What this movie actually covers are the final days prior to the death of this individual, and not the moment that he is thinking about it. *High Noon* is another effective demonstration of the fascinating possibilities of experimenting with time in film. In this movie, the clock becomes one of the principal elements, constantly appearing to confirm that the minute it shows coincides with the spectator's watch. It is not at all strange that the name of this movie, when shown to the Spanish-speaking public, was *A La Hora Señalada* (*At the Appointed Hour*). The effort of the director of this exceptional movie has but one obstacle: It is impossible to project at the same time, on the same screen–at least it isn't possible today–two or more actions developing simultaneously in different settings. Here we begin to see not only the possibility but also the necessity of a panoramic movie in the future with a mobile viewer. In this film Fred Zinneman gives a passionate tribute to the style of John Ford. He offers it in a way that only a true artist can, by contributing with his own creativity and showing the master that his teachings have suggested fascinating perspectives.

In all aspects of cinematography relating to creativity, Ford has been both forerunner and master. Knowing where to find the threads that are woven more deeply into the feelings of the human being, he communicated with the public through signs that go directly to the senses of the spectator. He does so without having to resort to banal explanations that only contribute to dampen the excitement we feel at having discovered something on our own. Every movie by Ford is a lesson on these principles. Ford's influence reached the most brilliant cinematographers: He was a mentor of Welles, Fellini, Kurosawa, Hawks, Huston, Stevens, and, in spite of the enormous differences between them, even Hitchcock. Italian Neo-Realism itself comes from a part of the essence and cinematic synthesis of Ford. The selection of scenes to give more clarity to the narration and continuity to the sequences, obtaining a greater emotional impact in the spectator, is one of the preoccupations of every director interested in making good movies. Without the need to present an enigma or alter his discourse, no one has known how to use these assets like Ford, with the dexterity he displayed.

* * *

Art and science, manifestations of the creative force of the human being, and sex, a vital and creative expression, form the disturbing trilogy over which religion attempts to establish its norms, with differing results in each. Political and religious powers frequently impose themselves upon the actions and liberties of man, but there is nothing they can do about the implacable force of nature. The sexual act is the only ceremony consecrated by all species. In harmony, nothing immoral can exist in it. Sometimes these are those who insist on associating morality with sex, seeing it only as something sinister and perverse. They are usually vile, ignorant or stupid individuals incapable of recognizing its glorious significance as the symbol of preservation of the species through ecstacy. By stigmatizing sex, they hope to make these natural acts an instrument of moral and religious principles. With cinema being the most powerful artistic expression of our time and the subject of sex one of its most frequent topics, clerics of all doctrines struggle to control one and establish some dominance over the other. Just as medieval artists and craftsmen found themselves obligated to include religion in their work, the modern-day motion picture producer, restricted by the puritanical vigilance of Will Hays, has had to accept censorship as part of his trade while getting the public accustomed to visualizing Eros behind the disguises imposed by Jehovah.

Censorship, even when implemented by governments, has its fundamental origin in religion. This makes sense, as the activities of the artist disturb the stability of religious institutions and their principles, which for centuries have also been undermined by scientific investigation. Science, in permanent evolution, indifferently continues about its labor, revealing with each discovery the fragility of dogma. The artistic community, more docile and malleable and–above all–less committed to the truth, has demonstrated itself prone to collaborating with the authorities in exchange for its patronage, while always threatening to go outside the dictates and the confines of religion. For these reasons, religion has remained in constant belligerency with science and art, and no doctrine has been too confident of the loyalty of the artist. We must be fair, though. Only half the violence practiced by man has its origins in religion; the other half is found within human nature. To put the creative force of humanity at their disposal, domesticate the imagination of man, and keep it at its mercy, thereby controlling the social activity of each individual, has been the concern and desire of religion throughout time. Before attempting to control the actions of humans, they had already invaded a more predictable field, establishing themselves as prophets and rulers of the forces of nature. One of them, sex, has from the start been the principal target of religious attention. Under the pretext of moralizing humanity, they have demonized this act that connects man with the rest of the living creatures. Dogma has demonstrated itself particularly fierce in anything relating to sex, and the religious power has more or less rigorously tried to impose its criteria on all the artistic expressions in which it has thought there might be some degree of sexual content. During the twentieth century, no other aspect of the arts was so closely observed by religion as cinema, and in an effort to maintain the essence of film intact, Ford invented an entire cinematographic language for this situation.

The public attention that film has received has made it the principal target of censorship, and this is not being done only by the church. Powerful groups have also joined the efforts in restricting the free exchange of ideas that creative activities offer humanity. Many are responsible for this and there are several ways of doing it, but nobody admits to it. There are much more effective ways of persecuting intellectual activity and trying to abolish freedom of thought than by burning books. To set thousands of piled books on fire in public is more than anything a symbolic act. What is truly effective is the prevention of the publication of books by harassing those who might risk their distribution. Of course, in both cases, the justification they provide for their pillaging activities is the pretext of saving us from ourselves. They pretend to protect us from dissolute ideas that could contaminate our thoughts. Nobody dares to point out that they do this with the purpose of defending their interests and institutions while, at the same time, keeping us ignorant of the crimes they have committed. Bureaucracies at the service of the powers that be, or influential groups close to it, are always conspiring against open criticism and the dissident individual in order to occult their insidious practices and shameful purposes. This is why the battle for freedom of expression never ends. Film has had to develop and evolve within this climate: Between science, which it finds indispensable and which helps it evolve, and censorship, which limits it and which it does not require. And it hasn't done too badly overall.

Life is only reality while it is happening;
it is illusion the moment we plan it,
and fiction when we remember it.

The yearning for communication that exists within human beings has through time driven the search of new forms of expression. Beginning with music, dancers facilitated the visual presence of sound through their movements. Following this desire for communication, primitive man conceived of the vocalization of ideas and gave sounds more accuracy through the use of words. That is how he finally arrived at descriptive literature, later on inventing metaphors that would bring about the discovery of poetry. This was not the only method used by humanity to express its concerns; the journey was guided by the judgment of the investigator and accompanied in its exploration by the imagination of the virtuoso capable of creating visual symbols. Working from a less abstract foundation than that of the poet in its desire to give volume to the images of the prehistoric painter, this last discipline gives birth to sculpture. The aesthetic passion of the human race reaches its maximum splendor during the classical period of our culture. It seems as if everything were art during Ancient Greece. Even the architect, the philosopher, and the historian were artists. Even so, it is in the twentieth century when, thanks to technology, human imagination conceives of the possibility of combining within a single activity all of the higher manifestations of its civilization. Artistic specialties came close to each other on occasion, but had never done so as an ensemble, nor could they be part of the same artistic expression as cinema now provides.

Science begins with the knowledge and experiences of the past and searches for an unexplored objective. Art also enriches itself with the contributions of culture, but the resulting work must be original. The scientist as much as the artist works with the thought of tackling the unknown; otherwise it is imitation, copy, repetition, or plagiary. Only those with creative minds are capable of producing ideas that can transform our environment or our way of thinking. A sign of the spiritual strength of a human being is the power to move and elevate thought in others. The field in which these exceptional beings toil can be determined by their natural inclination for a certain discipline or sometimes pure chance. The public classifies the different fields in which artists develop their work according to their experiences they identify with at that moment, without taking into consideration what the imagination of man might have in store for art in the future. An artist is defined by public recognition, not because they proclaim themselves as such. Their standing will be established by the depth of their thinking and the ability they might have to clearly transmit these thoughts, not by the means they use to express their ideas. Nowadays creative activity has possibilities of articulation unknown to our ancestors. Artists have remained the same; only the method of expression used to transmit the essence of their message has changed. Of the variety of available methods, film is the most recent art form.

More than any other art form, film is a limitless horizon open wide to the imagination. Its possibilities are boundless, the paths that can be followed in it numerous. Comedy, drama, thriller, etc., are all different directions that require a distinct approach in each case, but there are also the varied styles and resources employed by each director as he addresses the public. Lacking the necessary technical knowledge of the filmmaking process, I am going instead to refer to the impression that a completed movie produces in me. I can only imagine the techniques a director uses to compose the scenes he seeks. Whatever the merits of the artist, and the means at his disposal, the final purpose of art must be to make us feel the emotions and ideas with the same intensity felt by the one creating the work. For that, the director relies on a host of elements that make film a unique art. When these means are properly employed by a competent professional, the result is a good film. If it is also made with feeling, passion, and a deep knowledge of the human condition, then the film has emotional possibilities that are difficult to achieve with any other art form.

In music, the only truly abstract art, the spirit of the author surges from notes that need no explanation, containing as they do the essence of his being and his world. Cinema, in contrast, is an essentially rational discipline, a preconceived exercise where the impulses of the subconscious remain relatively hidden. However, aside from those that are shown to us as a logical sequence, the scenes and actions of characters in a film answer to unforeseen biological reactions. Background and development affect the character of the author, influence the unconscious decisions, and change the nature of his work. Both external and internal factors, indifferent to our wishes, are present in the activities of each being and determine our conduct. Who we are and what surrounds us is always changing, conditions that with supreme wisdom both Heraclitus and Seneca would assert: We cannot bathe twice in the same water of the river; no one is able to leap over his own shadow. Unless these principles are taken into consideration, it won't be possible to get very far into the analysis of artistic creation.

That which we have become through time determines our will; the world that we inhabit will limit our actions. In no other creative activity is this inevitability as evident as in cinema. It is no mistake that film is the closest thing to real life that man has conceived. Our religious and pagan dualities oblige us to observe each movie with diverse attitudes. These two tendencies saturate Western man's thinking and influence cinematic art. A narration where solutions are given on a whim, almost by divine fate, belongs to a messianic concept of culture and is pleasing to participants in–for lack of a better term–ideographic film. The other type of film derives from a pagan perception of the universe. It is more rational and analytical, placing greater influence in substance over style. The former relies more on technology and fashion; the latter requires a concept above all else. While one is the result of a collaboration of a large number of people, the other needs fewer resources to reach its objective; the idea is indispensable. These two tendencies could be summarized as an Apollonian inclination, which remains on the surface and prefers appearance while the other is more intellectual and penetrating, a sort of Dionysian cinema. The line separating one from the other might not be as clear as Nietzsche would have liked.

* * *

The movie audience represents virtually all cultures, and for each viewer, a movie will have different significance. But just as with any other artistic expression, only a certain minority will be able to grasp the deeper values of the work. For the majority of the public, movies possess attractions that, independently of their importance, are marginal to the quality of a film. As in painting, both the represented subject and the decorative value of the work seduce those who have scant knowledge of the purpose of the artwork. So, too, in film, an agreeable story told by way of pleasant images yet lacking much content, or an action movie superficially presented, can appear to many spectators as great masterpieces. This explains how weak paintings, as movies in the style of *Gone with the Wind* and the soap operas on television, have so many enthusiastic followers. Although in art no contentions should be scorned, some should be cleared up in order to avoid confusion and thus find the genuine virtues of a work. The better the comprehension, the greater satisfaction we will feel when perceiving its values through our senses.

Art–or at least excellence in art–is not within everyone's reach, and neither is creative ability. Perception of aesthetic values relies on factors that are difficult to describe. One of them, sensibility, is an indispensable condition to enable the thorough appreciation of a work of art and adopt the proper disposition with respect to the artist's intentions. Neither education, experience, nor the proximity of the object are of much help in artistic appreciation. Remaining in constant contact with art can provide us with a trivial knowledge of it but does not assure us of being able to perceive its essence. Film is not excluded from the phenomenon that causes art to be a rather undemocratic field nevertheless as its popularity increases; it becomes more vulgar and pedestrian. When some of those who participated in the filming of *La Strada* saw the finished product, they were disappointed. An agent in Hollywood claimed it was the worst movie he had ever seen. This moving film by Fellini is a simple and accessible story for anyone with a minimum of sensibility; even a child can appreciate that he is in the presence of a masterful work. Beauty is definitely not in the eye of the beholder. It is in the work itself, waiting to be discovered by some but not by everyone.

Art is produced from the awareness of an idea that the mind feels compelled to share. However, this process is not complete until whoever experiences it is capable of understanding its significance: It is a secret complicity between the artist and the public, a silent agreement of an aesthetic order. Conception, transmission, and reception are three equally important stages in the creative process. Without any one of these, a work of art will not be achieved. Film shares this characteristic, but it is also the only visual art destined for the masses. Without their support it would not be able to survive. That is why not only are the thoughts of the artist reflected in the film, to a certain extent so is the mentality of the people to whom it is directed. This is the reason why the origin of a movie is easily recognizable, even without taking note of the language of the dialogue. In each country, communication between the director of the movie and the public takes place through similar processes, with the aid of various techniques and disciplines that are more or less used in the same fashion. Consequently, it is not technology, or the location where the story is filmed or takes place that most influences the structure of the film. For example *Viva Zapata* by Kazan is easily recognizable as a product of Hollywood, yet it is much more realistic and completely different from the declamatory and solemn Mexican version on the same subject. The foremost determining factor of the character of each movie is the style of the director as well as the influence the public has on that movie director.

* * *

As a spectator of film I have been able to determine that feelings and ideas can be displayed in film only with the strength and passion that the director is capable of injecting into the movie. All the professionals who participate in its elaboration (actors, photographers, and assorted special technicians), although necessary, are only instruments the director uses to achieve his purpose. Throughout its history, the film industry has absorbed a great number of components from the rest of the arts. Music, dance, painting, sculpture, sound, etc., are all elements at the disposal of cinematography in a way no other art is capable of assimilating. However, film is not capable of being an instrument of the fine arts; it can only reflect and benefit from them. The era of musical comedies was one of the most fertile in the use of these resources. The directors of these films brought sound to the public not as an aid in understanding the plot and development of the film but as a catalyst of the show.

During the fifties, music and color came together as a creative impulse in Hollywood, and films of impressive beauty were produced. *Singin' in the Rain*, directed by Stanley Donen, is a choreographic display that captivated the public with the beat of its rhythm. The dances in this production are of incomparable visual impact. During those same years, the heart of America was brought to the screen with seductive charm through two movies that depicted different times: *Picnic*, by Joshua Logan, and *Showboat*, directed by James Whale. Both demonstrate an abundance of good taste, and their beauty and dynamism go beyond the possibilities of Broadway. The first is a tribute in color to the romantic spirit of youth. The second, an homage by Jerome Kern and Oscar Hammerstein, depicting the majesty of a river with a history, is a saga dedicated to those who have traveled down the Mississippi or who have approached her shores in reverence. Cinema finally appears to the public fully enriched by all other expressions in the fine arts.

A dazzling example of the utilization of other artistic disciplines within a movie is *Gigi*, where Vincent Minelli, in addition to choreography and music, adds scenes taken from Impressionist paintings of great masters. He introduces fine arts into the action for the first time and makes it work marvelously as a visual effect in the film. For example, when Gaston and Gigi make their entrance at Maxims, the background suddenly stands still referencing a painting by Renoir. The interiors of the movie are principally by Bonnard or Degas, and there is an amazing twilight by Toulouse-Lautrec which is seen in profile accompanied by only a romantic melody. Paintings by Monet, Manet, and Pissarro also help give the Belle Époque new life in this film. It is obvious that resources well-utilized can contribute to enhance a movie, but do not guarantee its excellence. For that, in addition to having great command of the craft, it is indispensable to possess deep feeling and to know how to passionately express it. It is entirely possible to produce a detestable movie using Dostoyevsky's best novel, music by Mozart, sculptures by Michelangelo, paintings by Raphael, and perhaps even the efficient performances of Sarah Bernhardt and Laurence Olivier. The difference will be demonstrated by whatever ability the director has to bring these marvels together.

The musical comedy has a short life, perhaps because the stimulating possibilities it offered were made common by television. Just as it alters people's lives, technology also influences their preferences, and the direct transmission of images to the viewer's home was going to have unpredictable effects on the psychology of the public. While music and dance dominated the cinematographic scenery, by the fifties television was growing in popularity and becoming colorized. As it learned from the cinema and benefited from its advancements, the designers of this revolutionary invention developed its own field of exploration. At the beginning, aside from live transmissions, it would only broadcast cinematic creations. As the viewer could watch these programs for free and commercials were the only source of income for the new industry, it was logical that producers would expend a great deal of creative effort in publicity. With a dependency on cinema, it wasn't long before glamorous dance routines from musicals, or inspired by them, where incorporated. Influenced by the movies, comedies adapted best to the taste of the television viewer and, consequently, music and dance represented the best supports for the commercial needs of this fledgling activity. The scenes on television that people saw while moving around in their homes had often been extracted directly from the movies, which now the whole family could see on the small screen while listening to the same music that up to then had only been heard inside the theater.

Throughout the day, viewers might watch a similar show while subjected to the same repertoire of musical commercials. With time, the remote control would come along to help, in some measure, to avoid being exposed to the repetitive intermittent commercials. As only natural, the public has stopped looking for that which, on occasions (though in a less attractive format), it was obligated to view during the day. That is how, as a consequence, while the spectator was abandoning his seat at the theater, the choreographer, dancer and singer took their talents from the big screen to television, where their efforts would be at the public's disposal at all hours of the day. There is nothing strange about musicals becoming victims of an environment that trivialized them, then put into competition with an industry that little by little separated it from its most inspired and enthusiastic creators. Technology deposed it and made the musical comedy only a memory. But perhaps with the advent of "high definition" on the panoramic screen, the same technology that made it languish might become the impulse that will bring back that delicious form of fantasy.

In spite of the discouraging panorama, every once in a while cinema attempts to bring musical comedies back to their former glory. The most recent effort is with the helpful resource of special effects. There are times when cinematic advances manage to supplement the talents of actors and actresses who only pretend to dance or sing melodies sung by others. The difference is difficult to tell, but it can be felt. Some of these musical attempts have come to the big screen recently, buoyed by a large publicity effort, even though the meager artistic value of these films cannot be disguised. Nonetheless, one of these luxurious productions was rewarded with an abundance of Oscars (trophies that are sometimes awarded for inspiration and more frequently for the lack thereof) a few years ago. Just when it appeared that music and dance would disappear from the leitmotiv of film, *De-Lovely* makes its appearance–so far the most suggestive film of the new century. With the subject being Cole Porter, his music, sophisticated lyrics, degrading promiscuity and general good taste in life, the director almost creates a miracle. This film is not a comedy, but a musical drama projected through well-timed flashbacks that contribute to give coherence to the storyline; a tale conjured up by evocative scenes that are evidence of an exuberant genius and inventive imagination. When staging the glamorous past of Porter, Irwin Winkler manages to create a new reality where memory remains alive and time is only a fascinating fantasy.

* * *

There are those who are scandalized at the image distorted by the capricious fantasy of a painter or reject the novel where the narration and description by the writer does not coincide with historical documents. To reproduce history is not the aim of the artist, but to use it. Events are only useful for the author as inspiration and will only be followed by him for as long as they are useful in obtaining the greatest effect for his images or within his narrative. In spite of this apathetic artistic disposition, the creative representation–even when it does not adjust to historical reality–will become part of history without consideration of whether the work is faithful to the document upon which it is based. Cinema is not privileged as far as the precarious relationship that art maintains with respect to truth. Since those of us who try to approach it do so from differing perspectives, truth, although intangible and severe, has a diverse relationship with each of the disciplines in which human thought develops its activities. Even though in the laboratory it is the inseparable companion of the scholar during his investigation, truth remains indifferent and distanced from the studio where the artist works. While it is invoked in the temple, truth is the implacable enemy feared by magic and religion. Truth's descendent, faithful server, and loyal confidant is honesty; dogma has also lived in perpetual conflict against it. Even so, it appears in Voltaire, Spinoza, Galileo.

To learn the psychological effect that an image can have–not on an individual, but on a large group–it is necessary to have remarkable intuition and an extraordinary knowledge of human essence. Great filmmakers have this ability to a large degree, and, without meaning to, have contributed in altering the tastes and habits of millions of people. Their indisputable influence on the public has essentially made film into a revolutionary art. Now that the past century of great changes has ended, in retrospect we can clearly appreciate that film has been the truly innovative art. We have seen a diversity of individuals parade past, publicly proclaiming ideas that pretended to transform the world but have only contributed in paralyzing a great portion of it, while movies actually changed our way of living. After a century of social speculations, science, through applied technologies, continues to be the great revolutionary, and film–perhaps for being intimately associated with it–has contributed to its influence.

The contribution of film to humanity has been enormous. Through movies we have gotten to know each other better, and distant countries have come within reach. Through its images we have been able to appreciate that, while the wishes and hopes of man may vary, this diversity should not necessarily produce antagonisms and confrontations. In the end, film has helped us understand the human race in its plurality, its different cultures, and to observe them with less prejudice. By making us understand and accept the habits and customs of other countries, cinematic art has created a significant change within society. Film has contributed–perhaps more than anything else has–to human coexistence, everything that all of those promising doctrines and political demagogues haven't been able to even inspire. Without comparison, more than any other artistic expression of the past century, film, along with the press, have been the great witnesses of our time.

Traveling down the road;
to carry within the light of the stars,
the songs of birds, the sparkle of dawn.

In his wonderful and erudite dissertation *Civilization*, Kenneth Clark underscores the testimonies left by man throughout time and provides us with a conduit to find the true significance of art: As he clearly states, art reveals the spirit of history. As always, its spirit–in music, sculpture, painting, literature, and now in film–can only be transmitted by a real genius. If art, in addition to being a creative expression, must also be a testimony of the time when it is produced, then nothing has reflected with greater realism the experiences, tribulations, and hopes of humanity during the twentieth century as film has. Of those who were fortunate enough to participate in this passionate adventure, many enjoyed the advantages of fleeting fame, but few were able to come close to the boundaries of glory. Others chose not to recognize the value of innovative creative effects in film or didn't know how to approach them, and saw only lucrative possibilities. Among those who understood the immense and promising field that was opening up to them, John Ford decided to explore the horizon with passion and stood guard throughout almost its entire history. During the 56 years of his career, of the 136 films that he directed, I have somewhat arbitrarily chosen those that have left the deepest impression on me. I am sure there are other films by this director that deserve the same attention, but I wanted to concentrate on those stories that have made me reflect intensely or on those which I remember best. My selection has also been influenced by my belief that these can give an approximate idea of the temperament and preferences of the director: Style is that which describes the character of a man, and his tendencies are what define him. Following the inclinations of his idiosyncrasies and adjusting himself to the norms of civilization to which he belongs, Ford has given life to his ideals through the characters he profiles. By elaborating upon an original form of expression, he has constructed a world for us. Outside of literature, no one has contributed as much as Ford to praise the independent and free spirit of the individual, or dedicated as much effort to building a monumental tribute to human solidarity.

The penetrating realism that John Ford projects on the screen is always convincing, but in the end, his representation is a subjective reality. What we are seeing are not only the situations as best as we can assimilate them, but also history the way he would have liked it to be. To make this ideal panorama plausible, not only must he make the scenery credible, the director must profile the images of the protagonists and explore their psychology in depth. This incisive approach to the characters and their surroundings is where Ford–clear yet profound at the same time–comes closer to Shakespeare than anyone ever has. To intimately portray someone implies going inside them, and whoever does this must also give of oneself in the representation. The characters will behave within the limited parameters that the script requires of them, but being indiscreet confidants, they will also reveal the convictions that the artist imparted on them during his visit. This is how Ford has reached many of us, and this is also how I would like to try to reach him–not through any properly defined critique or through an erudite examination of cinema, but through the content of his work and by risking an interpretation. Emulating the style of the director, I will attempt to articulate the impressions his movies have made on spectators. Each of his films contained images that penetrated my mind in the darkness of the theater, experiences that became a persistent part of a cosmography and that appear suddenly, tinted by memory. Perhaps in trying to be original, I have been a bit too optimistic by adopting a somewhat speculative system to foray into the films of John Ford. I hope this will not appear an extravagance. It is possible that the symbolism found in much of his work has many other implications, and surely his incisive style of representing the human condition requires extensive analysis. I am only trying to explain what some of the films of this intuitive director suggest, that which each movie provoked at the time of viewing or years later when remembering it. Powerful signs that nurtured my imagination back then and now make themselves known, perhaps a bit deformed by time. I want my mind to delve deeply into his thoughts and perhaps, without being equipped to do so, I am going to try to journey down a different road. I would like to be the first to travel through unexplored territory, even if I stumble with every step. It remains to be seen if I have been able to find John Ford at some point during this journey or if it has all been an illusion. Have I confused the fundamentals of his work or have I managed to understand his inspirational language? Shadows or light, whatever the results, there is an opening through which ego has slipped in. Although I am unable to illuminate his discourse with the precision that I yearn for, to me this will be a passionate mental adventure through the imagination of a genius.

*Action is the signal that starts the camera rolling,
and action is also the evidence of life.*

The Iron Horse – 1924

The Union Pacific Railway is constructed while
Davy Brandon searches for his father's assassin
and comes across his childhood friend Miriam
Marsh, the daughter of one of the owners of the
railway company. Miriam is engaged to Peter
Jesson, who works for Bauman, the true assassin.
Bauman and Jesson conspire to prevent the course
of the railway from going through a pass that
Brandon has discovered and to make him believe
that his father was killed by the chief of the
Cheyenne tribe.

When this film premiered, the movie studios where already involved in the
cultivation of stars of the silver screen destined to saturate the imagination
of the public. A system had begun that would give origin to the commercial
success of some of the most prosperous industries on the planet. The first
settlers of the Country of Illusion soon learned to shrewdly interpret the
wishes of the public, transforming the spectator's interest into obsession,
and as a result, an industry. Dazzled by the moving images, moviegoers
followed with admiration the almost mythological symbols that the
celluloid idols represented on film. John Ford preferred not to partake in
the benefits of glitter projected by these stars. The recognition his work
received never depended on the prestige of the actors and actresses who
participated in his movies. It is possible that at the beginning of his career,
these stars of the cinematic firmament were not available to him. In any
event, he did not want to merely film public celebrities from the roster of
the great studios, but to reproduce characters that had life only within the

story and whose emotions could be transmitted to the very core of the viewers. The creative possibilities that he discovered for the industry separated him from the strictly commercial purpose of producers, and from then on the films of Ford had their own inflection and finality, contrary to those laborious monopolies of success.

When cinema didn't yet realize it was mute, *The Iron Horse* finishes filming; the limits to silence were still unidentified. Three years later, animation acquired a voice, and, in the middle of a celebration shared by the rest of the world, Hollywood announces the synchronization of words to the vocal movements of actors. With spectacular effect and precarious artistic results, in 1927 cinema sings a song and speaks its first phrases. Even so, *The Jazz Singer* was purely a technological triumph. In spite of this, the first spoken movie caused a real commotion. Up to then, movies were a form of entertainment that the public appreciated as a lesser theatrical representation, but without great creative attributions or the cultural level they have today. In the early days of cinema, neither the public who supported it nor those who worked within the industry would concede that science had a place in the aesthetic. What may seem so clear now hadn't even been considered prior to the revolution of sound bringing about a deeper reflection upon the artistic virtues of the new spectacle. The possibilities that film promised surpassed the conventional notions of that time, subjected for centuries to the traditional forms of aesthetic expression: dance, painting, music, etc. A film of transparent celluloid that made images move was the beginning of a new formula for art, a form of expression that depended essentially on technology.

When I saw *The Iron Horse* for the first and only time in 1946, I was already familiar with the films of John Ford. By then, this movie was already considered old. He might have predicted the arrival of sound prior to beginning this silent film, because the movie's pace appears to be a premonition of the approaching acoustical novelty. Before the application of the new invention, through written dialogues reproduced on the silent screen, the public was able to follow the nature of the story that was developing. However, the reading of these texts distracted viewers who would lose concentration on the other visual symbols that were shown on the screen. To free the public from the need to read while watching a film was one of the great contributions offered by sound. The viewer could concentrate exclusively on the action while hearing the thoughts of the protagonists. Sound accomplished two different purposes unrelated to each other: Speech replaced the signs that would appear from time to time during a silent movie, generally explaining the motives of the characters and now, through this new resource, the director could consider the possibility of assigning speech a less explanatory function, making it more emotional, especially in scenes of greater intensity. The omission of dialogue, imperceptible in silent movies, becomes evident to the public during the course of these new talkies. By portioning out sound during the course of action, the new purpose of silence is discovered, whose paused application would become essential to cinema from then on. Phonetics provided a promising field to expressionistic cinematography and, when dialogues were introduced, Ford immediately realized that by introducing dialogue and extending pauses to their limits, the new effect could contribute to achieve greater emotion and eloquence within the scene. Shortly after *The Iron Horse* the new art would pursue its perfection and be comprised from then on by three known elements: sound, visual images, and silence.

In his movies filmed with sound but no dialogues, one can predict what the director will be able to achieve when the actors' conversation catches up to the action. In 1929 we hear for the first time the voices of the protagonists in *The Black Watch* and *Salute*, unveiling the dramatic impact of silence in a movie with sound. But the fundamentals of the language that he would establish with the introduction of acoustics had already been experienced in *The Iron Horse* and in a few of his other silent movies. Ford appears to realize from the beginning that the appeal of sound would not lessen in any way the visual qualities of cinema. The expressive force of film will always reside in the images, and this is something that no noise will ever be able to change. When Hollywood loudly proclaims to have created the miracle of sound, John Ford proves that movies should be made to be seen more than heard and finishes filming *Four Sons* which appears a year later. At the same time that the public was listening to the new idols of the silver screen, he decides to present without sound the vast range of feelings that are concentrated in this story. *Four Sons* is a revealing movie in more than one sense: This is his first antiwar film and it is also in defiance of the new talkies. In relating the suffering of the mother who sees her children sacrificed on the opposing battle lines of the same war, John Ford makes an eloquent and emotional declaration for peace that sound would not have been able to surpass. The psychological resources of this new cinema that he began using in *The Iron Horse* would allow him to perfect *The Informer*. With his silent movies he was able to give us an idea of what film might become when stimulated by sound. Even though he had already used sound effects in different films prior to this movie, he would wait years before adding speech and experimenting with dialogues. The feat realized by the American people in uniting the two oceans might have benefited by being narrated, but I assume it was not feasible for the director to repeat the theme, even if it would have been fascinating to compare both versions in terms of the same expressionism exposed to two different techniques. The transcontinental train served as the subject of numerous movies by other directors later on, but Ford didn't think it necessary to generate a spoken version of this epic. Perhaps he wanted to leave this film associated to the memory of *The Birth of a Nation*, the other pinnacle dramatic work in the history of silent movies in Hollywood.

Ford waited a while after directing this western before deciding to film his first talkies, and the plots of his first two movies with sound were much less ambitious. Even though the projection of that railroad feat would take all imaginable resources within his reach, he did not want to vocally repeat a movie that, in a certain sense (just like the movie by D.W. Griffith), is related to one of the great achievements of this nation. The noticeable influence this director had on him at the beginning of his career might have had something to do with the decision to leave his legendary *The Iron Horse* forever silent. Nonetheless, John Ford was destined to use this new resource like no one before him. Even though this was a movie without a voice, in it one can discern what his future films would be like: Even without dialogue, he manages to create significant pauses during the movie that suggest the intense communication between the protagonists. It might not have been noted by most at the beginning, but Ford discovered early on the capacity film has to transmit emotions through silent sequences. Before delving into movies with sound, he investigated the expressive possibilities of images, and in his last silent movies the influence of sound can be seen–and not just as a resource to facilitate the understanding of the story. Ford would make various silent films while the industry was concentrating on exploiting the rich vein of sound that technology had placed at their disposal. Perhaps he wanted to wait for the euphoria produced by this novelty to pass, and for a more serene disposition from the pubic toward this revolutionary invention. From the moment that it acquired the ability to speak, film became a part of the few artistic representations that can transmit their significance to more than one of our senses. This required certain adjustments by the director in the conception of the movie, as well as by the public adapting their sensibility to the impressions this new technology would transmit. Cinema as an expression has its limitations. It is only able to transmit the actions and emotions of the characters, but without being as prolific in explanation as a novel. Spectators needed time to assimilate these acoustic effects on their other senses.

Before D.W. Griffith began the ambitious project of narrating the beginning of American expansion in 1915, movie cameras had resisted narrating great historical events. A year after the premiere of *The Iron Horse*, Sergei Eisenstein would reproduce the dramatic event of the Russian Revolution in his *Battleship Potemkin*, carefully excluding any reference to the assassination of the Czar's family. Against the complacent disposition of the communist director towards the victorious, Griffith announces to the world the existence of the Ku Klux Klan with all of their ominous paraphernalia and grotesque theatrical display. America's harshest critics are Americans themselves. That is one of the things that makes this country so great. Reminiscent of the two films *The Birth of a Nation* and *Intolerance* and their critical intent, John Ford formulates a call to the white man's conscience with *The Iron Horse*. For some reason he even lets the Indians name this movie, at a time in Hollywood when films were being made in which Native Americans were considered barely human. According to the optimism of the new American, the 'iron horse' was an engineering advance that united one end of the country to the other. However, in the narration it was clear that for the forgotten victims of progress, it split their world in two. The progress of this industry is only a pretext and serves as a background. The story of the engineering achievement, the determination of a country, and the conflicts that arose during the assembly of the railway surpass the possibilities of any cinematographic drama. Cinema, like painting, can only reflect history in an anecdotal manner. Consequently, Ford reduces his story to one of the conflicted situations that could have taken place during the evolution of this gigantic undertaking. The movie only covers a fortuitous episode of that achievement. With a style that would set him apart from then on, he tells us of the adventures of ordinary persons that destiny has placed at an event worthy of remembrance.

After *The Iron Horse* there is another significant silent western by John Ford entitled *Three Bad Men*. In his films, these types of works appear to be associated with the optimism of the country. When things aren't going too well, the West will always be awaiting the American who decides to follow its path. The confrontations that take place on the western journey are usually the subjects of these movies, and their scenery is almost always the unlimited horizon and the geological monuments found along the way. All of the ingredients of the classic western can be found in *The Iron Horse*. As a background and testimony to history, this film features the landscape through which the railway was advancing and which many times served to inspire the imagination of the director. The drama develops alongside the construction of the transcontinental railroad, which President Lincoln decided to endorse. The protagonists are honesty and valor pitted against duplicity and the insidious. The plot has something to do with the project under development by Union Pacific, but not much. The main player in the conflict is Davy Brandon who belongs to that breed of intrepid risk-takers who have made possible humanity's great achievements. On the other side is Peter Jesson, mendacious and opportunistic, who pretends to defend the interests of the railroad company when he really works for Bauman, who is against the train tracks going through the pass that Davy has discovered. Jesson manages to convince Brandon that the death of his father was brought about by the chief of the Cheyenne tribe, knowing it was Bauman who actually killed him. This is the essence of the antagonism that gives rise to the interchanges narrated by John Ford with his characteristic clarity. The story has a happy outcome, as is the custom of this type of episode: The intrigues of Jesson do not have the end results he hoped for, nor does he manage to keep Miriam Marsh away from Davy. When the railroad lines meet, Davy is finally able to join his childhood girlfriend.

More than any other, this movie deserves to be examined in relation to the time in which it was produced. In later films, Ford will examine more directly the drama of the Native Americans, but in *The Iron Horse*, he already makes note of the abuse to which they had been subjected. From then on, in each of his films in which Indians appear, John Ford does not ask for compassion, only respect. History shows us that invaders sometimes manage to commit misdeeds while attributing the responsibility for their crimes to those they have defeated. During the time in which *The Iron Horse* was filmed, individuals of other races were mere tools in Hollywood. Their feelings weren't worthy of being portrayed in cinema. In this film, as in many others, Ford showed how the privileged position of those in power allowed them to attribute to the weak, crimes they did not commit. This story by Ford forms part of the condemnation which would become more widely used in film. It draws attention to blame unjustly attributed to the Indians by the unscrupulous and greedy. It was also an invitation to examine the tragic situation that the advances of our technology were causing in the life of this country's indigenous people. Bauman commits a criminal act against the honor of the Cheyenne chief, but his dignity is admirably restored when the slander is discovered. This episode represents the director's solidarity with the Indians when treated unfairly.

The Iron Horse awakens our curiosity as to the other offenses the insidious have been able to ascribe throughout history to those who have not had the opportunity to defend themselves. By designating the Indian chief as the innocent victim of the deceptions committed by the powerful white man, it is a call to bring us closer to the indigenous world of that time and to reflect on the context in which the conflict took place. By then, more than a century of history verified that the relationship between these two peoples had evolved without either culture ever managing to understand each other. There were profound impediments that began with a nearly opposite view of man's place in the universe, which made mutual comprehension even more difficult. The main obstacle to a better understanding began with his arrival, when the white man felt himself the owner of the ground on which he stood. To the Indian this was an inconceivable illusion and an outrage that offended his dignity. Not everything had been aggression in the past: One hundred years earlier the existence of Native Americans had been enriched by the contact with their new neighbors, making it more dynamic with the help of the horse provided by the white man. To the admiration of their teachers, these skillful horsemen learned how to ride with amazing expertise. But this new ironclad instrument was not within reach of those nomadic tribes. It only fulfilled the purposes of the European man, who used it against them without taking into account the needs of the Indians. To the Indians, the 'iron horse' was an intractable moving fortress they were powerless to oppose. This steel monster interrupted the migration of the herds they were accustomed to following while settling their camps nearby. The railway line was like a bloody open wound that flowed to the horizon. Protected on the platforms, some of the passengers would decimate the buffalo herds and, on occasion, entertain themselves by shooting directly at the Indians. Those who classified the Indians as savages conducted themselves with inexcusable brutality, and only the ignorance of these senseless invaders could provide some sort of explanation. The technology of the white man placed the Indians at a disadvantage when it came time to settle the growing conflicts; the intractable horse had sealed their fate.

The accusation Ford makes against those who feel they have the right to commit misdeeds under society's protective cover becomes a constant from his very first films. The common moral denominator of his movies is the defense of dignity, when those in power abuse their authority. This theme appears to be fundamental to the ethics in almost all of his stories. As far as the conflicts that affect the characters, he doesn't adhere to any particular doctrine and tries to keep his personal or religious preferences at a distance. He rejects falsehoods and abjection. He identifies with noble purposes and admires the determination shown by individuals defending their principles. It is these steadfast fundamentals of conduct that he respects, revealing his romantic inclinations and the humanism of a movie director who stands firm in his convictions. Inconsistency isn't very cinematographic. To remain true to one's norms and principles against the majority always implies a risk. Even so, to realize a work that is worth something, it is not enough to be a virtuoso motivator of effortless applause; you must be able to invest something personal.

The Informer – 1935

> In exchange for enough money that will allow him
> to leave for America with his girlfriend, Gypo
> Nolan betrays his best friend by informing the
> police of the whereabouts of Frankie McPhillips,
> which gets Frankie killed. Gypo spends the night
> wandering through the streets of Dublin until he is
> executed by the Irish Republican Army, and dies in
> a church at the feet of McPhillips' mother.

My first encounter with John Ford occurs with a strange movie. A man of primitive and brutish mentality wanders through the night unable to escape his remorse. Ford understands him compassionately in spite of his infamy; it is the others who judge him. He finds something inside this being that is worthy of redemption. It is his own conscience that eventually betrays and destroys the informer. This entire psychological plot is transmitted with surprising clarity through images. The sound in this movie is vague, like shadows in the background or the chorus in a Greek tragedy. The sequences that precede the end of the movie are strikingly dramatic. All that is heard are shots being fired then Gypo crosses the plaza and drags himself to the interior of the church. There is an intense exchange of stares between him and the mother of his victim–a dramatic silent dialogue–at the same time comprehensible to the entire audience. It is the ruination of a being that finds himself too late, a drama with traces of indulgent and delicate humor.

The cheerful sentimentality of John Ford is clear to me in this dramatic episode of an embattled Ireland. As in some of his other plots, he warns us that life observed in small doses usually appears as a comedy, but when contemplated in its entirety, it can only be presented as a tragedy. When I first saw this movie I was about ten years old, but I knew that I had discovered something new. I returned home both thrilled and happy. At that time, I used to go to the movies occasionally without my mother. I suspect that this was because she applied the money for her ticket to more important things. It was customary for me to describe the scenes in detail while she cooked or ironed in the kitchen of our home in Bilbao. That night, before beginning my narrative, I was so excited I was only able to say, "I can't explain this movie–you have to see it for yourself." I didn't think I could describe the sensation of having come so close to the drama. I felt that the essential significance of the movie would be beyond my narrative powers. It was as though I had discovered a new dimension in film. Perhaps personal circumstances might have contributed to stimulate my senses during that time. An uncle of mine–brother of my mother–was hiding at our house and would climb inside the coal bin when the doorbell rang, emerging later with a blackened face. Back then the police would make frequent raids, in search of more-or less-active dissidents. Consequently, I was familiar with the ambiance depicted in the film I had just seen. I was able to perceive subtle details in the film that under other circumstances might have gone by unnoticed. *The Informer* was a revelation to me. This film made me realize that movies are not only an art form, but an intense and profound experience for the spectator. I realized that in film just about everything is possible, if the director has sufficient talent.

The Informer marks the birth of modern cinema. Everything about this film is innovative: the approach given to the storyline, the rhythm of its development, and its outcome. It is reasonable to believe that Orson Welles had the main character of this movie in mind when he conceived of his "Citizen." We can recognize the similarities between the two individuals, even as opposite as they are in their aspirations and so different in their backgrounds. During the last moments of his life, Gypo becomes aware of his mistakes through an emotional process, while Kane realizes the banality of his ambition when his death is imminent. Frustration identifies and unites them. During a moment in each of their lives, both succumb to an obsession and they choose desire over higher reasons for being. Ford makes this clear through the compassion with which he treats the subject, and Welles reveals the same intention in real life when he tells Randolph Hearst that Mr. Kane would have liked the movie, if he had had a chance to see it. In the end, a feeling of immense failure burdened the characters created by each of these visionaries, who form part of the chosen few that have influenced film since then. After them came Stanley Kubrick, Robert Aldrich, and all the anti-hero genre of the sixties, which the Actors Studio stars glamorized so successfully.

Through logic and reasoning, Kane can foresee the consequences of his actions and has the faculty to discern between the causes and effects of his impulses. By reviewing his life, his intellectual condition could not reach any other conclusion than the one Welles takes for granted. Conversely, Gypo is only capable of learning through experience. The regret springs forth as suddenly as the impulse of his betrayal. The idea reaches him like a diabolical revelation. Ford makes us watch the awakening of the traitor's conscience, in the only way that he is capable of perceiving the horror of his action–through trivial nocturnal encounters that allow the informer to establish an inner dialogue with himself, brief experiences, but of intimate significance Gypo's subconscious: The blind man who appears to have witnessed his intentions, or the reward banner for the capture of his friend, which he violently rips from the wall, or the poster that stubbornly chases him until it sticks to his body, and while he tries to remove it from his leg, he hears a sweet

Irish melody sung by a street tenor. That is how the mind of a simple man becomes conscious of his infamy and faces the dilemma between loyalty and the desire that drove him to disgrace. Orson Welles resorted to a much more complicated being to represent this internal conflict. His greatest merit consists of being able to produce a movie on this same dilemma, yet so different in all other aspects.

The central characters of these two masterful works have a literary background but are nonetheless almost exclusively cinematic creations. *The Informer* was extracted from a novel Ford used to develop the drama and placed Gypo in the circumstances that allowed him to reach to the depth of his being. *Citizen Kane* is based on reports, commentaries, and references to a press tycoon who had become a public celebrity. Prior to being given prominence by these two films, both existed mostly in the imagination of the readers. The lack of psychological definition gave Ford and Welles considerable freedom in the creation of the characters. They almost carried out a clinical analysis while exposing the subconscious of these personalities. In both films, the spectator is able to observe the plot and its development through the confused and tormented minds of these two individuals. What Gypo and Kane feel and think is fundamental to these movies; everything else is background material that serves as scenery to emphasize the profile of each character. In film, the possibility of carrying out the personal creation of the director becomes more difficult when relying on great literature. Dostoyevsky, Shakespeare, Stendhal, or Cervantes leave little to add when describing the characters and their human situations. Ford has avoided this limitation by refusing to use texts by these authors. Orson Welles, less intuitive but perhaps more cultured, defies this obstacle by searching for intimate nuances in literary works and trying to project the essence of the discovery already made by the writer. However, he paid dearly for his audacity. His exploits led to interminable editing, and left him without the backing of producers, forcing him on a sad pilgrimage in search of funds to finance his movies. But *Citizen Kane* was not made during this period of his literary investigations. Welles made this movie when he found in Ford the teacher that came closest to his restless and creative imagination.

Citizen Kane is a deep intellectual assessment of the acute psychological intuition displayed by Ford in *The Informer*. Welles demonstrates that moral disaster is not the consequence of Gypo's brutality, but an indirect consequence of Man's obsessive nature, which can be found in all levels of society. Charles Foster Kane was educated to succeed, to sweep aside whoever got in the way, and no one would punish him for his behavior. The other is a loser unprepared to face the decision he has so suddenly taken. Even in Gypo's world, an action of this kind is not allowed. At the expense of his honor and without even considering the consequences of his actions, Gypo forgets the loyalty he owes his people and exchanges it for passage to America, thereby freeing himself from the oppressive situation that impedes his dreams. On the other hand, it wasn't the search for freedom that encouraged Kane's plans, but the desire for dominion and to exert control over fellow beings. He does so by sacrificing the love and respect of those he forgot during his unscrupulous march towards power. In the end, from different paths, each character discovers that life means little without that which each decided to ignore. They reach the painful conclusion that, for personal gain, they have sacrificed the beings and feelings that are most worthy of respect. The disgrace of a single act or systematic predatory conduct brings them to the same conclusion. An ignorant being, nearly oblivious, commits a tragic error. The other, better educated, pursues a misguided obsession during his entire existence. Both end in the saddest manner that a human being can: Looking at themselves with contempt.

It's not about making qualitative comparisons between these two films; Great works of genius are made to be improved upon. Mediocre films have no positive destiny. Welles and Ford were both conscious of the nurturing condition in culture, which is why they admired each other and were in agreement in their cinematic conclusions. In a strict moral sense, these two films complement each other by illustrating the different possibilities in which obsession develops. The first portrays a single night, while the other chronicles an entire life. Irony emerges in the comparison between these two characters: One more intelligent and developed, realizing the error of his ways in the years past, and the other, less educated, must regret the damage caused during a single instant of weakness and confusion. Between the two we learn that whatever the origin of a disturbing desire or the intention that encourages it, identical effects can happen to the life of a primitive individual or to a more sophisticated being. To the depth that jealousy, indecision, or adolescent love has been described by Shakespeare's pen, we can now add the brilliant exposé of the obsessive human condition made by these giants of cinematography more than three hundred years later.

Mary of Scotland – 1936

The story of Mary betrayed by her husband and
executed by order of the queen. The love affair
between Mary and Lord Bothwell. Elizabeth's hate
of the other aspirant to the English throne.

The cinema of Ford is comprised of imagination, intuition, and fantasy.
Literature helps him create the ambiance of a scene and helps him remain
faithful to the essence of the narration. In everything else he feels free to
create a new reality and present his own vision. In an unprecedented effort for
him, he attempts to film characters that were historically distanced from him,
and in doing so puts his imagination to the test in a field for which only
historical references are available. By undertaking such a distant subject in
history, it prevents him from being able to dig deep into the beings he must
imagine. The common denominator of his other movies is that we always see
images and situations that are close by or, in certain cases, part of his
background. Before and after this film, the emotions and intensity of the
drama in a story have always been the result of the sagacity with which he is
able to delve into beings that are more or less close to him, but the three
centuries that separate him from Elizabeth of England and Mary Stuart is too
much time to penetrate the collective or individual psychology of the
protagonists. The common understanding by Ford of the idiosyncrasies of
these characters requires an intimacy with them that is not possible, and
consequently, *Mary of Scotland* is not the best movie this director realized. To
identify with the tribulations of each individual, a chronicler needs to come
close to what he is relating, otherwise the story might have some
documentary value, but it will lack strength.

In some measure almost all of the films by Ford have something to do with
his personal experiences. He knew soldiers who fought in the Civil War and,
through them, he must have had the opportunity to hear revealing anecdotes
on the character of generals leading the armies and the human condition of

the president. Under the moonlight, he shared the frugal meals of cowboys and reflected next to the pioneers on their progress through the desert sands. He had the opportunity to hear from Wyatt Earp about his passage through Tombstone, to hear from his lips the dramatic episode at the O.K. Corral and learn how the sheriff planned his deadly strategy. In his youth, he might have had the chance to meet Irish leaders in New England who dominated the American political panorama during the first part of the century. It is also possible that some of the patriots that fought for Ireland's independence might have known previous generations of his family. Literature intellectualized the mind of John Ford, but it didn't prevent him from searching for knowledge from the personal experiences of American Indians who inspired him, and whom he got to know almost as well as Sam Peckinpah did. Ford wanted to transmit to us the history of four generations that he observed up close and make us participate in the feelings and emotions of those who formed part of his story. He knew that to truly understand events one had to experience the reversals and joys of the protagonists. Otherwise, the narration would suffer. For this film, the director invents characters and, with the help of history, imagines their surroundings. He observes them from a distance, which is why *Mary of Scotland* is not one of John Ford's more realistic films, but it has other attributes that perhaps will allow us to better know its author.

External forces contributed to limiting the development of the subject matter in all of its passionate components. Apparently orders from the powers that be limited the possibilities of this movie, and we all know depth is not often found within the grasp of film producers. We can imagine the investors deciding it to be more commercially viable to give the film the epic aspect it deserved to have within history, but Ford preferred to delve within these two women to give their struggle an essentially emotional character within that historical conflict. The director has a right to do this. The imagination of an artist can use any event from the past without surrendering to the historian's rhetoric, because for a work to have any validity it is necessary for the style of the creator to remain intact. Film is not an art where explanations can be extensive. The ideas must be transmitted through visual impressions and brief discourse. What goes through the minds of the characters is not projected on the screen or explained in detail. The emotions of the protagonists can only reach the public's heart through symbolic images. This film is relevant to John Ford's career for more than one reason. In addition to being his only film that takes place during the sixteenth century, in it the director clearly states his ethical convictions. After *Mary of Scotland* the inconformity of Ford's personality towards established values will become more evident and his films will frequently question the privileged, who have no other virtue than the ability to adjust themselves to social conventions. To make this disposition of his more obvious, three years after *Mary of Scotland*, the heroes of his narrative will be an outlaw and a prostitute. John Ford's righteous spirit reacts against the establishment that serves only as a cover for the insidious and to give respectability to miserable beings. His discourse in favor of the individual willing to defend his rights and the freedom of others is the leitmotiv of almost all of his movies. His heroes are simple men and women resolved to protect honor and family with their lives, certain that the justice of their mission is above the maliciousness of those who seek to humiliate them. The characters of his movies are indifferent to both slander and flattery and are unconcerned if their noble purposes are not immediately recognized. In the Ford cinema, nobility is more frequently found among individuals who are not particularly concerned with protecting their own reputations, and the generous spirits he idealizes live inside people who are usually rejected by those privileged by fortune.

Ford is not a director of spectacular decoration or imaginative superficialities. What he is interested in are the ideas that inhabit the mind of the characters and inspire their impulses. In *Mary of Scotland* it is the internal world of the two women that inspires the director and, in spite of the difficulties that time places on being able to penetrate the psychology of these people, Ford stubbornly attempts to delve into the characters of the two protagonists. Elizabeth, virginal and a Puritan, appears insensible and evil, in complete contrast to the innocent purity that the sensual Mary projects. Ford prefers to believe that Mary was tortured and sacrificed for her sexuality rather than any political motives or for reasons of the State. To give this supposition more sense, he emphasizes the psychopathic aspect of the sovereign, and although he might have taken certain liberties with history, there is no doubt that he intuitively gets it right in many of his observations. Knowing that perversity is more frequently found among those of repressed sensuality, he profiles a queen who is incapable of reconciling her own happiness, the joys of life, and well-being of others with the monarchy. Elizabeth's behavior contradicts that which religion preaches, but history has shown that her deeds are very much in keeping with the practices of the church. Ford avoids sinking into the religious theme–a requisite subject in the movie–preferring to place emphasis on the difference in temperament that exists between the two women: The sexuality of one in contrast to the spiteful coldness of the other. Some of the great literary works have had these antagonistic factors at their core, and certain authors have studied in depth how environments contribute in aggravating a certain disposition. There is no doubt that being the only Moor of stature in Venice is a circumstance that contributes to exacerbating Othello's jealousy and making it uncontrollable. The reading of novels that tell of the adventures of traveling horsemen sublimate Alonso Quijano's schizophrenia until he becomes Don Quixote de la Mancha. Shakespeare also tells us that there are temperaments that are prone to giving rise to certain tendencies. Hamlet's depressive condition has origins in his lack of decisiveness. This psychological reaction, in John Ford's story, against the sexuality and stoicism of Stuart increases the queen's hate and, in spite of–or because of–her religious condition, Elizabeth lashes out with homicidal rage against defenseless Mary.

In each of his movies Ford endeavors to make evident the human condition of the characters, at the same time, whenever necessary he emphasizes the incompatibility that might exist between them. These two females created by John Ford are dispositions and perhaps even biological opposites, but not anomalies of the feminine soul. They are frequently found within the human species, and when they encounter each other, the only mission of one is to destroy the other. Mary's conduct is consistent in relation to the feelings that drive her, in contrast to the duplicity of the queen, whose behavior varies according to what her interests and resentments are at the time. Faithful to her principles, Elizabeth lets herself believe that she is acting in the interests of the State, but the hate for Mary's sensual and reproductive richness is genetic. This moral incongruity is not rare among the followers of any faith. Through time, doctrines have had little effect on the conduct of individuals. Then and now, jails brim with criminals who declare themselves believers. The best thing that can be said about religion is that it has not contributed in any way to elevate the morality of its followers. The religiousness of the queen rather than her political abilities is reflected in the image of Elizabeth created by Ford, and her actions are more conditioned by her biological reactions than subjected to the interests of the monarchy. Acute observer of the human condition, he must have realized that without the experience of maternity and especially without the practice of sex, a woman can become an irascible animal, dangerous and cruel. With this sovereign figure, he creates a type of woman psychiatry should study more in depth. John Ford's films are full of opposing personalities, and he makes Mary Stuart a voluptuous near-goddess, in comparison to the morbid coldness of Elizabeth. Even so, this queen has passed into history as the great political figure of her time: The woman of State willing to sacrifice whatever was necessary to assure survival of the empire. In the movie there is no mention of the implications for the crown, the religious convulsions in Ireland, Wales, Scotland, and of course England. Empires can only be sustained when there is a strong metropolis with a satisfied beltway, as the historical queen knew well. Advantaged disciple of Machiavelli, she manipulated or eliminated with equal ability those who surrounded her if this would bring about a positive result for the monarchy. Ford sidesteps this pragmatic disposition of Elizabeth in order to concentrate more on her biological reactions. For the director's purposes, it is necessary to make the queen an emotionally unstable female, since rational practices in politics contradicts the visceral impulses that in the film are attributed to this sovereign.

Her religious condition does not prevent the queen from lying, slandering, and vilifying Mary's image. Nobody is going to censure her behavior, because in dogma's semantic games, perversion is usually given sanctity, and within the strict dominion of religion, romanticism can be considered heresy. The religious morality does not condemn those who act in benefit of the ecclesiastical hierarchy, nor does the law punish those who defend the interests of the State. According to history, Elizabeth takes advantage of this condition of the clergy to protect the stability of the crown, but according to the movie, her actions are less rational and more to satisfy her instincts as a female rejected by nature. The intolerant and messianic temperament of the queen designed by Ford finds a better fit within the Oriental esotericism rather than Western rationality. This has a somewhat contradictory significance with respect to history: A fanatical sovereign would not have easily become part of the iconography of a country that gave the world the Magna Carta. The religious harvests acclaimed by the English populace have almost always come from the minds of dissident clerics. In the medieval era faith took possession of the language to manipulate concepts and, when convenient, to confuse terms, but the tendency in England toward freedom of expression created over time a permanent obstacle to this purpose of the church. For those who inhabit the theocratic areas of thought, words are sacred by providence's design, and only in advantage of its interests do they have any value. Only God's voice inspires the religion that supports the bloody excursions in defense of faith, remains implacable against freedom of expression, and is scandalized by blasphemy. Even so, those conscious inheritors of Western culture can honor their principles and their word without having to rely on divine will. Some stigmatize or destroy those who dare to express doubts of the validity of dogma, while others are better prepared–without renouncing their norms of conduct–to accept the discrepancies and coexist with those who are believers. Two positions that have been in constant confrontation since the arrival of monotheism, symbolized now by an usurper queen and the legitimate heir to the throne, who will remain defenseless as it is in neither the interests of the church nor the crown that her voice be heard. The secretive and mystical temperament of Elizabeth effortlessly accommodates the demands of faith, and Mary's sexuality responds more to the forces of nature.

Ever since man has walked this earth, he has been incapable of doing anything worthwhile if his actions held no passion. Even so, the passages of time chronicle events that have been inspired by baser sentiments. History is a collective memory; life observed in retrospective allows us to learn how we have become who we are. It is living in the present while examining the past in the opposite direction. It leads us to the most edifying way of accepting the reality of our existence. By studying the experiences that for centuries have either advanced the human mind or at times made it lapse, we learn how to face the future. History is useful for this and many other things. Everything our ancestors did has an effect on what we do today, so no matter how free our thinking is, it is impossible to ignore the force that dogma continues to represent. Two thousand years of Christianity is a lot of time to reject the religious influence in our past and even in the present. Through this offended queen, the doctrine reveals once again its absolutist vocation and exhibits its Oriental origin, messianic and cruel. The belief of serving God oftentimes drives the torturous acts of the clerics. The complacency of the populace that allows this is what makes possible their evil mission. They all contradict nature's designs, which is indifferent to human will and which certainly does not share the superstitions of this arrogant and egomaniacal monkey that is man. Ford echoes the liberal trend that begins to develop in the eighteenth century and through *Mary of Scotland* questions the clerical legitimacy. However, this is not an anti-religious movie, but rather a cold and distant view of this subject. Recently, as the church has lost some of its strength, cinema has tackled some of the more risky themes of the monastic life. In this century, through *The Magdalene Sisters*, Peter Mullan makes a devastating critique against the position of the church with respect to sex and faults an entire town of religious insensitivity and clerical cruelty. This fabulous European movie shows us how those who believe they are in good standing with God can also demonstrate a terrifying insensibility when inspired by the fanaticism that faith provides. The process they follow is always the same: First they proclaim their superior moral condition, believing themselves to be anointed by divine will, and, finally, they convince the rest that their disgraceful purposes are inspired by providence. This is how, by unifying wills that without the official proclamation of dogma would remain scattered, religious activity materializes into a formidable instrument in favor of both repression and war. Pacifist in appearance, religion pronounces itself against violence; nonetheless it has been the biggest instigator of almost all of the warlike actions in the past two thousand years of history. The powers that be conspire to alter or cover up the past, but history–or more or less accurate interpretation–continues to be at the disposal of anyone seeking to learn.

In essence, these two women could represent common Christians of medieval Europe who began to clash during the Renaissance. The religious context which the old continent was developing could not have been more confusing, even without considering the small pagan cores that were resisting conversion to the doctrine. A hundred years earlier the decomposition of the church begins, leaving behind centuries of darkness and opening a crack through which the light of free thought filtered in. In the meantime Christianity had disintegrated into irreconcilable factions, deeply involved in Byzantine discussions that only searched for the most effective way to proselytize. Inside this climate, each sect had begun its own particular type of persecution against the others and, in certain cases, these disputes would last centuries. Fifteen hundred years earlier the church had begun its sacred mission of destroying man's ability to reason, repressing his curiosity, limiting the investigations by wise men, and almost suppressing human creativity. When they thought they had given uniformity to human imagination and stability to the spirit, the disturbingly glorious Renaissance began. It was the awakening of Europe from its lethargy. Even from the very first centuries of our existence, the clash between the values of Greece, rational and philosophical in the face of Oriental provincialism, had not been demonstrated with so much violence. Like the symbols of the two cultures that coexist in Europe, the opposing images of these two women are the representation of this conflict. It is a fortunate coincidence for the director that the name of one of them is of Middle Eastern and biblical origin while the other comes to Christianity from the polytheistic past of the old continent. In both cases, the names fit the symbolism that the film has assigned to them: "Elizabeth" is

Hebrew in source and its image and messianic origin appear to be torn from the bible. "Mary" corresponds or is similar in sound to that of a character of pagan mythology cultivated by ancient Europeans. The ethnic diversity of their names is an allegory of the different human conditions of these two women and reflects the distinct temperament of each. The instincts that guided these women in real life might have been distorted in the story, and perhaps the protagonists of this drama are only imaginary compositions by the director, but the symbolic structure of the film is consistent with history. It is possible that the personalities of these two historic figures might not have been as defined as Ford presents them, and it is certain that their images were altered for cinematic purposes. We also know that during their respective existences they were subjected to circumstances that are not evident in the film, but the final outcome made possible by this moment in time coincides with the intentions of director of this movie. Mary's sensuality, which exacerbated Elizabeth's hatred, is extinguished with her life, but Stuart's fertility survives the monarchical destiny of the sterile queen.

Stagecoach – 1939

Ringo, a fugitive from justice, joins a group of
travelers crossing New Mexico in a carriage and
ends up falling in love with Dallas, one of the
occupants of the vehicle. During the journey they
are attacked by Indians and one of the passengers
dies. Upon arrival in Lordsburg, Ringo kills the
assassin of his brother in a duel. In spite of this, the
Marshall lets him escape to Mexico with Dallas.

The open spaces of the American West encouraged informality, sheltering under its
skies individuals from some of the most diverse social conditions. The men and
women who traveled across that geography did not pay much attention to the
Victorian restrictions of those times. This carriage is almost a microcosm of the
human disparity that was spreading throughout those territories, and each of the
characters traveling in it has a symbolic equivalent in the external world and our
imagination. The situations they experience during their journey condition the
reactions and behavior of the travelers, and represent the diversity of individuals
that could fit the interior of a stagecoach. An outlaw and a prostitute are bundled
next to Henry Gatewood, a prominent citizen of the community, owner of the local
bank and furnished with the respectability that money provides. A prosperous and
established society is personified by this disdainful and thieving banker, and he
represents the visible part of the conventional values approved by most people. He
attends religious services and steals. This wealthy passenger has soared to a social
position the rest will never achieve and is indifferent to the feelings of the others. It
does not cross his mind to sacrifice his comfort for those who to him are only
insignificant traveling companions. Next to him, Peacock, the liquor salesman,
appears to have fallen from the sky to one of the other passengers, a providential
apparition in the opinion of Doc Boone, humorist, iconoclast, and drunk. In spite of
his shortcomings, this medic has more sense than all of the other companions, and
one can always count on his advice and experience. The carriage also transports the
idyllic dream that is in the heart of Hatfield, a gambler, stoic and fatalistic, willing
to risk it all on one card or a dame who captures his attention…until his romantic

illusion is interrupted by death. Next to this unusual personality, a metaphor for life, is the woman who will become a mother during the journey, and the inspiration of platonic love in the gambler. Birth from the fertile young body of Lucy Mallory shows us that existence must follow its course, even in the most dangerous of situations. The unforeseen event gives energy and optimism to everyone except Mr. Gatewood, who, in his egotism, lost the significance that man's journey through this world must have. Dallas, the female whom fate has treated badly, finds herself involved in the maternity of the other woman and finally sees her wretched youth redeemed in the eyes of the other travelers. She discovers her future and her hope in Ringo, the fugitive from justice that the carriage picks up at one point of the journey. This daring and lawless young man is the most artificial and least complete of all the characters in the vehicle, as Ford decided to make his image the epitome of the impetuous force. Those in charge of transport gave no guarantees of delivering to their destination this assortment of passengers–filled with self-denial, uncertainty, and hope. Adapted to the circumstances and the landscape, Marshall Curly is an example of what firm and benevolent authority should be. Next to him, whip in hand, is Buck, the conductor of the stagecoach, who follows the Marshall's instructions and hopes the travelers know what they are doing.

In addition to being a precursor to a more realistic and descriptive type of western, *Stagecoach* is a suggestive work of art. Sound made it easier to introduce more subjective elements into the vitality that these types of movies already had and made it possible to enrich the feeling of the story. Ford glimpses the possibilities of the cinematic narration and creates an adventure film that has great social significance and penetrating psychological value. In its journey from Tonto to Lordsburg, the human cargo aboard this carriage is exposed to a series of adventures that test the resistance of the travelers. The director manages to completely capture the attention of the viewer with the setbacks during the trip as well as the differences that arise between the passengers. A mutual need keeps them together during the dangers and difficulties that arise, and predispose them to confide sentiments that in other circumstances would remain unspoken. By reflecting the emotions experienced by the protagonists during the journey and revealing the moral condition of each, John Ford's carriage is transformed into a setting where the cast of characters he has imagined acquire lives of their own. Nothing that occurs during the film is gratuitous and everything responds to the symbolism that the narrator wanted to bring to our attention. The end of the voyage is enlightening. The banker gets an unexpected welcome and must console himself that the ladies, who would ordinarily have greeted him with smiles and flattery, ignore him this time to focus their attention on one of the fellow travelers. These ladies of the community look upon Dallas with contempt; they are offended that she does not share their same sordid aspirations. With the brief appearance of these arrogant matrons, it is as if John Ford is trying to give emphasis to this type of female, unyielding and devout, who disdains self-denial and sacrifice and hates a woman capable of risking her well-being for something that might have a higher meaning. This scene leads us to think that perhaps some of the more offended ones might be hiding a degrading past, and we wonder if maybe one of them

might be where she is now after having once been an obliging madame. All of these hypocrites and obsequious ladies deep down have the mentality of a frustrated Messalina. There is nothing more puritanical than a woman of dubious reputation determined to hide her past.

The western is modernized by *Stagecoach*, and from then on its components become part of other genre in cinema. In spite of being a classic among the films that portray the odyssey of the American West, it has been a model for directors of dramatic and adventure films unrelated to the world of the cowboy. The evolution that is perceived in *Stagecoach* from earlier films happens without the movie losing one iota of its Western heritage. Each of the elements that compose this genre is included: cowboys, the dramatic chase, the presence of the law, the duel, and the obligatory idyllic ending. There is no lack of open spaces that invite meditation, or the interior of a tavern full of smoke and life sometimes interrupted by the pistol shot. The camera takes us through the desert panorama of Monument Valley, a landscape animated by Indians on horseback and the fast carriages that crossed it desperately on the run. This is a patented formula in the westerns by John Ford that would go on to be incorporated into the movies of other directors, who, with the help of technology, have not stopped to this day from making it more spectacular and lucrative. In addition to the facets of action and suspense in the film, *Stagecoach* includes for the future of the western scenes that were once the exclusive prerogative of dramas or that until then had only formed part of another type of more sentimental movie.

Sound had been around for more than ten years, and it appeared as though all conceivable technical applications had been exhausted, but the dramatic possibilities of acoustics had barely begun to be explored. A few directors with imagination had discovered that the emotional effects of sound transcended the purely explanatory purpose of dialogues, but westerns had only started to experiment. Under the restrictions imposed by silence in the cinema, it would have been impossible to offer the spectator the expressionist innovations that would characterize John Ford's films from this moment forward. In this movie the sound is not only heard, in one of the scenes it is also a protagonist. Ford experiments with one of the episodes in the story that did not fit the traditional western: He keeps the camera focused on the interior of the tavern while the duel takes place outside so that its outcome is not visible, but the public can nonetheless hear the gunshots. This was completely opposite to what had been done previously. In the typical western, the death of the defiant villain by a revolver shot is the culminating point of the movie. In *Stagecoach* the dramatic effect of the choreography of the duel in front of the audience, something almost obligatory in cowboy movies, has been eliminated. During this scene the action is imagined through the use of sound, but the end result is nothing but conjecture, which changes from one instant to the next. The conclusion is portrayed by the figure that makes his entrance during those interminable seconds, only to collapse to the floor of the saloon: The still-living image of one of the Plummer brothers gives the momentary impression that the duel did not have the expected result. This western responded to a whole pattern of prearranged results. Even so, from the start of the movie it was apparent something had changed with *Stagecoach*. The final outcome was the expected one–just as in other movies of this type–but the sequence of events had changed, producing an uncertainty that would forever characterize suspense cinema. The viewers were not indifferent this time to the fall of the villain, since a few seconds earlier his presence had signaled the demise of the hero. This imaginary sequence with the purpose of intensifying the dramatic effect in a scene was later used in a variety of ways by many others, although Hitchcock was the one who did it best.

Behind its appearance as an insignificant western, there is profound significance in every aspect of *Stagecoach*. Those who want to classify it as a film of no importance that achieved only an immediate success confuse simplicity with superficiality. The work of an artist capable of creating something substantial through understandable symbols without having to recur to subterfuge contradicts those who search for a metaphysical meaning in art, usually with the only purpose of hiding their ignorance or covering up their ineptitude. The world is plagued by individuals determined to show depth, who spend their lives unnecessarily complicating things so that in the end they can continue to be as frivolous as always. Ford produced *Stagecoach* following the route already outlined by him for these stories of the American West, and with a clear but incisive style gave the movie the dynamism the public expected. The film created a movement that has been followed by many other movie directors, but it also spawned some bad imitations that became almost as well known as this movie. The success of this western awakened the greed of certain producers, who (as usual) were unable to go beyond the superficial in an attempt to repeat the anecdotal and fake the content. Fortunately, this film also captured the interest of true artists who figured out how to effectively incorporate John Ford's teachings into their work. To point out each of the films where traces of *Stagecoach* can be found would take forever. But of those, *Hombre* comes closest to the essence of the masterly film by Ford. Fortunately, it is also one of the most honest and suggestive stories that has been presented about a group of people traveling in the reduced confines of a carriage. The director of *Hombre* realized that John Ford had left the most prominent protagonist of *Stagecoach* unfinished, and where others only saw opportunity, Martin Ritt finds inspiration. In this omission by Ford, he finds a whole world to explore and profiles one of the most interesting characters that has ever been shown on the silver screen. The most relevant distinction between the two movies is that during Ritt's narration, everything revolves around Hombre, while in *Stagecoach*,

Ringo needs to relate to the other characters. The former is patient, capable, and calculating; the latter is bold, athletic, and audacious. Their characters are different as well, according to the style of each director. Even though one of these cinematic sketches is born as a consequence of the other, only the carriage and its accessories are the common items in the two films.

Even though Martin Ritt managed to create an incomparable character, *Hombre* premieres with little success in 1967. This singular man is different from all the ones we had seen before, but as real as any person who crosses the street or is seated across from us during a train ride. The director of *Hombre* finds the atmosphere for his story in Ford's film, but plunges us into completely new circumstances from those in *Stagecoach*. The intention of delving into the psychology of the travelers is evident in both narrators, and the two films give life to characters that we get to know quite well. *Stagecoach* and *Hombre* explore the reactions of various individuals to different conditions during the journey through scenery that is unknown to some. The diversity of the characters as well as the unforeseen situations they face is the subject matter for both of these extraordinary movies. The essence of these films is found in the clear delineation of the protagonists; the carriage only rolls along and makes both stories unfold. The similarities between the external components of each story and the configuration of both movies are obvious. There is a coincidence in the expressionistic intention that Ford and Ritt both demonstrate, but also a large disparity in the characters that each invents and a fascinating and original approach with respect to the situations presented in each movie. One of the most notable differences in the main protagonists of each story is how they confront danger. Ringo finds himself within the interior of the carriage, in the company of people who know him and that he understands. He knows the way his neighbors will react to a particular situation and which of them he can trust. Conversely, Hombre is not comfortable next to the other passengers. He believes he cannot trust any of them, and only beyond the small space of the carriage does he feel in his element. *Stagecoach* is John Ford's optimism taken to the extreme. Ringo is by nature a man of action–he doesn't believe in the need to ponder things much–while Hombre is a reflective being who considers all the possibilities before taking any decision. Even so, his life ends before the conclusion of the journey, while Ford makes his hero survive. In Ritt's movie there is a Homeric element to the voyage. Even the relationship between the married couple traveling in the carriage has a tragic premonition. The screams of the wife beseeching her husband's help appear to be clamoring for

Sophocles rather than Hombre's daring actions…even as he is moved by the laments of someone who disdains him. Female protests full of bad omens pull Hombre to the ill-fated end he had predicted.

Hombre personifies two antagonistic worlds within the same person. He believes he understands the white man but is sure that he will never be understood by them. He is an individual indifferent to the opinions of the other passengers. This disdain for the others and his calculating disposition give him the appearance of invulnerable strategist. He considers the land to be Indian country and knows they are better prepared to survive in those surroundings. Aware of the consequences, he has decided to be an Indian and feels that should he ever abandon his people, nature and fortune will go against him. If he lets that happen, the gods will no longer protect him, the horizon will darken, and his enemies will beset him hidden by the shadows. In the world of the white man, he has the advantage of his European features. However, he does not want to adapt within a society that scorns his people. Everything would be in his favor in the white man's world. Even so, he effortlessly manages to let the Indian in him prevail in his appearance. This land demands something more than good intentions to survive on its surface, and Hombre believes that, should he ever forget this, he will be lost and predicts that if he ever relies on someone who doesn't understand this reality, it will be the last day of his life. The limited space of the carriage does not allow his dexterity and survival abilities to be of any use, so that during the trip there is no opportunity to know his capacity. One step outside the coach and the skillfulness of his abilities would immediately be evident. Strong and resistant, he only has one moment of weakness when he lets the romanticism that comes from his European half to prevail over the stoic disposition provided by his Indian blood. Without much conviction, he confides in the most honest, young, and sensible of his companions, and in a heroic gesture of human solidarity, he finds himself face to face with the death that was awaiting him. He dies when he risks going against the murderous snares he anticipated. It wasn't his skill that failed, but his luck. He is destroyed by the good intentions of someone in whom for a single instant he entrusted his life. He was not in any predicament. What induced him to take that risk was something he recognized in himself and that, until then, he had planned to reject. He wanted to cross the threshold that leads to European paganism by its most dangerous path and falls victim to the romantic impulse that encourages those who live within it. In the end he is seduced by the siren call that makes him forget who he is and falls like a mythological Greek god. That is how Martin Ritt made *Stagecoach* roll once again down the old roads of the American West thirty years later–with *Hombre*.

Young Mr. Lincoln – 1939

Abraham Lincoln begins his career as a lawyer and
embarks upon his first romantic relations. He
obtains a victory in court by representing two
individuals accused of murder and demonstrating
their innocence.

The relationship between history and art can only be fortuitous. They meet at
certain points of their itineraries, in moments necessary for one and convenient for
the latter, but they have never quite been able to be in agreement with each other.
The historian stumbles upon art during the process of investigation, and the artist
uses history in the manner most convenient to his creative purpose. History
gathers evidence and testimonies, directly or deformed by transcendental events,
and usually pays tribute to or stigmatizes the protagonists. If it could be written
without the intervention of the human being, it would be unquestionable. The
problem is that it is written by man, and interests and passions become part of the
diverse historical interpretations that time has accumulated. History is a fluid but
incomplete archive as well as an arrogant and authoritarian chronicle in that the
episodes, individuals, and anecdotes that aren't recorded cease to exist.
Conversely, for the artist history is only a point of reference that nourishes art with
that which it remembers as well as what it has forgotten. Gestures, details, the
inconsequential phrase that a historian rejects, are sustenance to the imagination of
an artist. These odds and ends of history help the writer and the illustrator to
create something worthy of being transmitted to the minds of others. To art
everything is useful and, like a diner with a resilient digestive tract, it feeds from
delicacies as well as trash. The beautiful and the repulsive, the greatness of a
heroic gesture to degrading human sordidness, they all serve the same purpose.
Scenery, experiences, sounds, and emotions come from all four points of the
compass to the work of the musician, choreographer, poet, sculptor, or movie
director. They accept inspiration from wherever it comes, and moral, social, or
historical classifications do not limit their activities. The resulting work can be
directed to a select group of connoisseurs or to delighted masses of society, but
during the creative process, art saturates itself from the plebeian depths of our

countries. Shepherds and anonymous troubadours inspired the first symphonic compositions with their accounts, and common folk have had a notable influence on music in all times. Renaissance paintings with celestial titles were in reality portraits of ordinary women, and, on occasion, prostitutes representing Madonnas. Drunks who frequented the neighborhood in Naples served as models to Jose de Ribera in paintings that supposedly represented the images of saints or ancient philosophers. This mystification became less necessary as the power of the church lessened. When art freed itself from religious dictatorship, the painter and sculptor adapted perfectly to the new symbols and various subject matters of the times. Literature has been less faithful to the dictates of power, and in order to give more freedom to his imagination, the novelist frequently alters events to free fantasy from dependence upon history. The more valiant, like the genial Bard of Avon, have been sufficiently encouraged to defy it. In any case, for the novel, the tragedy or the drama, a historical document can only serve as inspiration, not as the trajectory of the story. In all of its manifestations, art refuses to be subjected to the dictates of any other human activity. But as a capricious parasite, it reserves the right to borrow from all. Cinema, perhaps more than any other creative profession, partakes of the advantages and privileges granted by art. The director can take a subject from wherever and feel free to manipulate it to his whim. For a movie to have significance, the moving image that reaches out to us from the silver screen does not have to have documentary importance, and as for quality, it doesn't matter if the events reproduced in the film are transcendental or trivial. The value of the work will never depend upon the social position of the characters, the historic relevance of the sequence of events, or the accuracy with which the narrative follows the text.

In his eagerness to demystify history, Ford presents Abraham Lincoln as a more real and more human personality than Gettysburg suggests. The main protagonist of one of the most dramatic episodes experienced by this nation is portrayed in this film by inconsequential trivial anecdotes. The narration ends precisely before some of the most significant events in the lifetime of this country take place. One of these episodes would bloody America's ground and the other tragic event would end the life of this president. When directing *Young Mr. Lincoln* John Ford had no intention of filming a historic passage, but rather of describing the ambiance of the country prior to the ill-fated war. Everything that would end up having transcendental consequences for the future of American society is left out of the account. Perhaps he didn't want to meddle with that violent and painful chapter of

American history because war is a setting that makes little distinction between its victims, and Ford was an explorer of individuality. The director transmits the image of Abraham Lincoln before these eventualities of his presidency and entertains himself with those details of the life of the young lawyer who ordinarily would never have passed into history. However, by profiling his character he converts the personality of the future president into a powerful instrument of persuasion. Patriotic and optimistic, perhaps John Ford thought that this war did not conform to the principles under which these United States were conceived. The conflict between those who share the same country, ideals, and common aspirations makes this war an even more painful memory that is not easy for cinematography to explain. Through his films, Ford makes an effort to highlight the human condition of the protagonists through a code that offers almost as much significance to what appears on screen as to what does not. To understand his intentions, perhaps we need to speculate on the reasons he excludes the most significant portion of Lincoln's biography from the movie, and it might be necessary to pay attention to that which does not appear in the film. It is possible he might have rejected the idea of covering the war because he was more interested in describing the pacifist disposition of the future leader, and he preferred to contemplate this hopeful person without adornment or legends. He didn't wish to show the effigy flagellated by war. The young optimist that Ford places within our reach is far from the pained appearance Lincoln had during the last years of his life. The tragedy of the Civil War was to have reflected in the sad and weary expression that appeared in his eyes. Lincoln's countenance when he was president did not resemble that of any of his contemporaries. After that war between fellow countrymen there wasn't the smallest trace of optimism in his face. Wars are never celebrated by those who have suffered in them, only by those with no experience.

The Civil War was a significant catastrophe of incalculable proportions for the United States. Without the extensive territorial reserves offered by the Wild West, the country might not have survived this disaster. Two portions of the nation, with different economic structures, participated in the common colonizing enterprise and became involved in one of the bloodiest conflicts registered in history. The reasons were numerous, but the divisions were well-defined: Citizens that encouraged free and fluid migration entered into conflict with an exclusive society whose economy was dependent on slavery. The possibility of avoiding this confrontation is not worth commenting upon; it has already been examined by everyone interested in our history. Ford studied the episodes of the bloody war and probably also knew veterans who fought in both armies. He could not have remained indifferent after hearing their stories. Affected by all this, perhaps he inwardly lamented that the same emancipating result couldn't have been obtained without resorting to aggression. Two conclusions become apparent to anyone who has observed the violent episodes of history and who wishes these hadn't happened: Political genius is in obtaining the desired results without the need to use violence, and if–as they say–politics is the prevention of war, then war becomes the failure of politics. It is evident that John Ford did not want to represent the man he respected so much during the regrettable political fiasco. Neither can we expect from him the intention to glamorize the most painful episode of American history. In *The Horse Soldiers*, a later film, he demonstrated how painful it was for his imagination as an American to contemplate the country divided for nearly a year of its early existence.

His considerable sensibility allows John Ford to be a contemporary of every era that he portrays, to share the joys of those he films, or to offer his support during their painful experiences. The work of this director is essentially optimistic and always suggests a more romantic and less blood-thirsty solution for the aggressive reactions of our existence. Ford doesn't try to hide the reality of the struggle for life, but wishes to give this fate a less egotistical and more fruitful sense. He appears to think that since conflict is inevitable, all that is left is the dignified aspiration to put our violent instincts at the service of better causes. His work tells us that to declare oneself a pacifist in the abstract is as banal as proclaiming an opposition to the laws of nature. The existence of all species is founded on violence; a creature doesn't kill for any other reason but out of necessity. Man cannot withdraw from the conditions imposed upon him by nature. Civilization and politics only attenuate or somewhat regulate the natural human tendency towards aggression. Ford contemplates and makes us reflect. There is something positive in this: Upon reaching the moral point of his discourse, our thoughts do not conform to phony and easy solutions on the inevitable dilemma of die or kill. This is where John Ford's tolerant disposition towards violence comes from, and it can be accepted or rejected–according to the character of the viewer–but the ethical value it contains should not be spurned. The citizen, from the comfort of his home or seated in a restaurant, dedicates the gastric juices of his digestive system to convert some of the flora and fauna of this planet into excrement, might ignore and even deny the significance of his actions; that his life is an act of violence. But to give some sense to his ideals, a governor must recognize this principle. Politics is negotiating the divergence so that the aggressive human condition does not work against its own species. Nonetheless, sometimes events exceed the abilities of a leader and take him down paths that he might never have wished to travel. It is possible that Ford did not see a victory but a political failure in the outcome of this conflict between countrymen, and wished to place Lincoln outside of the disturbing scenery of war.

The film attempts to penetrate into the psychology of the man who would initiate a new humanism on which America would base its future. Ford wants to show us the country's condition before Lincoln's political formation, and what were the ideals that led to his electoral triumph and the calamity of war. The movie is far from being a drama. The discrepancies that would take the nation to violence had not surfaced yet, and the tragic events that occur during the saddest period of the United States were not yet in the minds of the protagonists. America was confidently on a destiny of expansion and prosperity that had not been interrupted since its inception. Ford describes the identification of Lincoln with the ideals of the nation through the spontaneous and sincere disposition of the young politician and the romanticism that encouraged him to share his experiences with the people. With admirable realism, the director replicates the context of a society satisfied with its liberty, a country that inherited the optimism and resolution found in the spirit of the pioneer. There isn't the slightest attempt at solemnity in the story. The trial where the new lawyer displays his oratory talents takes place in an informal environment, where humor is one of the most accentuated protagonists. The legal scenes in the film are the precursors to the numerous movies Hollywood has based on the court of law. Through the anecdotal, Ford wants us to understand the president that left a deep print in the history of this country and presents him to us during a period when myth had not yet consecrated his image. He wishes us to see Lincoln outside of government, a casual young man, optimistic and tolerant, as no one had envisioned him before. Perhaps this is how he best liked this American president of the nineteenth century.

The Grapes of Wrath – 1940

Portrait of the Great Depression shown through the
Joad family. Their journey from Oklahoma through
New Mexico and Arizona. Upon arrival in
California, Tom Joad must escape to avoid being
captured by the police.

If an artist limits himself to representing his own concerns, the work will be an intimate testimonial of his ideas. But when speaking for an entire nation, the result achieves the value of a historical document. The latter is only possible if the author does not give in to outside interests and rejects any influences from those who pursue a doctrinarian purpose. We know that Ford belongs to a type of narrator who does not play with the truth, but simply presents it without using it for any predetermined cause. So many twist it to fit their purposes that history tends to end up disfigured. Which is why, to come closer to reality, the more honest prefer to resort to their imagination. This time Ford decided to follow the path of Steinbeck and give movement to the drama that his novel recounts. The writer and filmmaker have created a testimonial whose veracity–contrary to historical text–nobody can question. The Great Depression has had commentators from all levels of culture, but no one has portrayed it in motion with the force with which John Ford does in *The Grapes of Wrath*. Ford dispenses with everything incidental and false that inevitably accompanies a legend, to give a credible sensation of the period while avoiding political clichés, because his work must be original. He speaks for every American who lived during those ill-fated years that passed so slowly during the thirties. His report is much more truthful than the fiery self-serving discourses of that time, and much more realistic than all of the promises made by the politicians, when pressed for an explanation of the crisis. This made *The Grapes of Wrath* a controversial movie and an incisive document, with its own journey through history.

Starting with the economic depression that assaulted the booming American industry during a part of the last century, John Ford puts in evidence the fragility of social institutions when compared with the solidity of the family structure. In the limited context of a group of beings united by misfortune, he summarizes the drama of an entire nation. Through a misery we can almost touch, he makes us aware of the distressing situation in which a large sector of American society was struggling during those years. In the circumstances produced by this disaster, Ford sees an opportunity to observe the reactions of man under adverse conditions. His conclusions are free of the partiality that typified the analysts of that time, who tried to find the cause in the effects of the catastrophe and put these faulty deductions at the service of their doctrine. Indifferent to these maneuvers, he shows us deeper feelings in the human heart that allows it to overcome adversity and misery. He emphasizes maternal sacrifice above all and the safe haven that exists in the family bosom. The instances of sacrifice that we see during the unfortunate exodus of the Joads persuade us of the existence of those higher values. As misery weakens social solidarity, we watch how intimate ties strengthen, and we foresee that the same man, who could kill for a piece of bread, is also capable of giving his life for someone. These are some of the reflections that the content of this movie suggests, but its message has many other implications. For those of us who were touched in some way by the effects of this crisis, *The Grapes of Wrath* is a living testimonial of those years of adversity. For those fortunate to only know the benefits of prosperity, this film is an impressive and realistic report of a painful but educational chapter in history. In finding this brilliant chronicler, the Great Depression made possible a masterpiece of cinematography.

In some measure, an entire generation suffered the effects of the crisis. So when John Ford narrates the odyssey of the Joad family, it was not difficult for us to identify with their misery. This association leads us to think about what might have contributed to the wounding of the American optimism, sinking a large part of this nation into poverty. One cannot think about this film without reflecting upon the reasons for the economic collapse and feel the temptation to speculate on its causes. When watching this movie now, there is no one in the darkness of the theater who will not wonder at the origin of that economic catastrophe, whose corrosive effects contributed to the destruction of so many lives. The misery caused by the withdrawal of capital, fearing the new socialist ideas, had devastating effects to even the most valuable and productive levels of the country and forced starving and out-of-work beings to wander in search of any means of survival. To some, the crisis signaled the collapse of capitalism. The "victim of its own internal contradictions" had begun its decline and was in its death rattle. For those who distrusted the Marxist verbiage, it was the lack of resolution by the government in facing the demands of socialism that caused capital, with its fear of communism threat, to retreat and abandon the productive sector to its fate.

Speculating on the origins of this catastrophe and what provoked it brings us to the field of economics. *The Grapes of Wrath* does not allow us to avoid this. Every person with intuition is wary of the explanations that the professional ideologues have given us over the years, so it is better to follow the rhetoric of two famous scholars on productivity. John Maynard Keynes and Milton Friedman do not contradict each other, as certain amateur economics enthusiasts claim. The strategies of Keynes were put into practice within a society in decline, beaten down by misery and in recession. Even worse, his sociological ideas were applied through a completely unproductive entity: The government with its characteristic bureaucratic inefficiency stepped in and tried to replace the fleeing capital. Friedman, who is also a philosopher, states that with the exclusion of politics from the economy this type of situation cannot happen again. His ideas are focused on the increase of production, and he maintains that the dynamics of prosperity are the best guarantees for the well-being of the country. He requires the reduction of the expense of government and rejects as inefficient its protectionist positions favoring any sector of society. According to Friedman's reasoning, granting charity with the money of others as bureaucracy does, is not philanthropy but a hypocritical form of corruption. In other words, he recommends the exact opposite of what the Roosevelt administration did during the crisis. The two proposals are not incompatible; they are designed for different situations. Under the same circumstances, it is quite possible that both economists would have been in agreement. Even if we doubt everything else, we can conclude that decisions taken by the government might have helped alleviate an economic disaster, but in this case could also have contributed to aggravate it.

Without addressing the origins of the crisis, Steinbeck and Ford send Tom Joad and his family out West, just as many years earlier America began its march toward its frontiers, but this time on a much less optimistic trip. In search of a better destiny, the Joads discover the animosity of the organized laborer who believes his interests are threatened. He feels no compassion for his fellow man, sees them as enemies, and harasses them. In his movie, Ford abstains from assigning blame to any particular sector of society. He doesn't even try to analyze the causes of the disaster. He simply films the effects on the faces of the characters. He does not participate in the feigned adulation political professionals use to approach the public, nor is he pleased by the glorification socialism makes of people as a herd. On the contrary, he simply observes the behavior of man, accepting the limitations that nature imposes on the human being and the possibilities that freedom offers. His sympathy is not for the amorphous masses, recipient of all the praises of bureaucracy, but for the anonymous individual, who manages to overcome adverse circumstances with his own efforts.

If we want to make an analysis that is not superficial on the importance of this film, it is essential to refer to the context in which it came about. Even though the movie was not made with that intention, it is necessary to point out its political transcendence and the influence that it exerted on the public at that time. *The Grapes of Wrath* is filmed during the days when the Second World War had already begun in Europe, which is why its distribution took place many years later, and the concepts suggested by the film were only fully confronted at the end of the war. After the struggle, socialism, which in Eastern Europe was showing all signs of evolving into communism, ended up becoming a bureaucracy, disappointing many of its supporters. However, the impracticable Marxist manifestos continued to be articles of faith to its followers, and the Bolshevik apparatus spread its propaganda across the planet with an efficiency that must have been the envy of Madison Avenue. Much more than capitalism, Marxism–as all other doctrines–hated and feared competition. Its attacks were predominantly directed against men of free spirit who honestly searched to build a more just society. In the popular arena, communists the world over battled to exterminate the cooperative movement, which was the most rational and promising representation of the worker prior to the war. After the war, they launched their pack of hounds against all the intellectuals on the planet who dared to question the legitimacy and efficiency of the "dictatorship of the proletariat," to give a name to the Soviet bureaucratic structure. At the beginning, an attempt was made to use the social conflict that the film exposes to give greater consistency to their theories. But beyond these maneuvers, *The Grapes of Wrath* is a virile chant of protest against the establishment, the equivalent of a political indictment that calls into question all of the proletarian utopias. Ford was branded a bourgeois as long as the communist propaganda lasted. In the Soviet Union, movies were being made that were so innocuous and complacent that they appeared to be the product of the Catholic or Anglican Church. We now know that there is nothing more reactionary than socialism put into practice, but after the war, this insidious propaganda had the effect of confusing many. The political importance of this movie has increased as time has passed, and its validity contrasts with the undeniable failure of those who made an effort to discredit its author.

From its creation, Marxism labored in disseminating an assortment of promises and nonsense that appealed to the ears of the masses; a demagoguery that also sought to obtain the support of certain minorities fiercely persecuted in Eastern Europe during that time. Everything that did not fit with their political purposes was destined to be stigmatized by Marx's disciples. But, as it often happens with fallacies, time was also against the communist dogma and the insidious critics of Ford. At the higher levels of thought, the political prestige of Marxism was in decline and had already been classified by some as another religious sect. Philosophers like Bertrand Russell, José Ortega y Gasset, and many others questioned its social effectiveness and pointed out Marx's mistakes for not taking into consideration, while developing his theories, neither nature nor the impulses to which the human beings owe their reactions. Inside the popular sector, distrust began to manifest itself, and every day it became harder for socialism to obtain the support of the working class. It is important to note that from the beginning, communist organizations had a difficult time recruiting followers among workers in the cattle and farming industries. It isn't easy to imagine a man of the country trusting socialism. Close contact with nature makes farmers more realistic and intuitive, difficult to seduce with social panaceas. There were some circles in the arts where communism increased its influence. They had Picasso and other painters and writers, but cinema was what attracted their attention most–through its extensive circulation it was easier to establish contact with the masses. *The Grapes of Wrath* was precisely what they did not want.

It is true that during the course of the film, offensive irregularities can be glimpsed that serve as criticism against the capitalist conscience. But inside their context there are also some disquieting aspects for fans of the philanthropic state. Without straying from Ford's stance of social assessment, the human factors that influence every social conflict are introduced in *The Grapes of Wrath*. With irrefutable realism, Ford demonstrates that the behavior of the proletariat under certain circumstances does not adjust to the expectations foreseen by Lenin's followers. The doubts that certain intellectuals had already expressed are for the first time within reach of the public through this film. It was being discovered that a bureaucracy–like any other parasite–is only encouraged by instinct to fatten and expand. The common source of doctrines was a subject of debate, and admittedly often changed the dynamic of history, but had never been able to improve the nature of man nor alter his human condition. As we know, economic theories–even if unworkable–can stimulate free thought in search of political solutions…as long as hustlers do not manipulate them. They don't care that their proposals–prior to achieving any kind of solution for the nation–must overcome in practice the difficulties of opposing perspectives and the diversity of personal interests that each individual will continue to defend. The dilemma is clearly presented to Tom Joad, a fighter for the syndicate who suddenly–without knowing how–finds himself facing off against the strikers whom he would have supported under other circumstances. This is how John Ford gives visual presence and actualizes the conflicts that dogma wants to explain by resorting to varied abstractions. After seeing this movie, someone might wonder if John Ford is an artist with sharp intuition, then Karl Marx might only be a practical joker with no sense of humor.

This is an absolutely visual film that has to be felt with the eyes wide open. A film that is economical in words and prolific in images, almost exuberant if it weren't for the sobriety of the style Ford has employed during his extended career. The concise nature of his dialogues matches the situations that the characters are experiencing. In this, more than in any other of his movies, Ford intends to prove film, although an audiovisual art, is made fundamentally for the eyes. This affirmation seems so obvious it might appear irrelevant, but if we compare his insistence in transmitting the content of a movie through an image, in contrast with the inclination by other directors to orally explain, we discover this observation is not as gratuitous as it might appear. While a movie by Ford is understandable if we plug our ears, a film by Woody Allen, for example, would collapse if the actors refrained from talking for five minutes. Silence in Ford cinema is almost always of a surprisingly emotional and eloquent nature. On the other hand, the most valuable part of Allen's films is the ingenious dialogue. The entire plot of some of the movies by this particular director could be followed with eyes closed, without missing anything particularly significant. Woody Allen's background in radio might partly explain this deficiency and abuse he makes of oral exchanges. It appears that the lack of visual sensibility by this master of obsessive trivialities, obvious declarations, and incessant dialogue leads him to express himself better through a continuous conversation between the protagonists. This observation makes sense when considering Orson Welles, who also came from radio. When faced with film, however, he instinctively felt the need to transmit his thoughts through emotionally moving and unforgettable images.

Ford crafts this film meticulously, taking care that every detail gives an exact idea of the magnitude of the drama. The appearance of the characters and their surroundings faithfully corresponds to the wretchedness of the situation. Ford knows that these scenes have to compete with all of the political literature of that era striving to give a false version of reality and the causes that shaped it. He doesn't try for a gigantic production or to include the entire nation under crisis, as Cecil B. de Mille might have. Ford only has half a dozen people represent all of the victims of this tragedy. There had never been a movie whose scenes had greater expressive quality. Nothing that we can imagine can produce a sensation of realism comparable to what we experience during this movie. The images of this film are of a deep and unbeatable poignancy. Nightfall, a pair of hands, an inanimate object or a face–everything responds to a question or silently formulates one. Desperation and resignation are represented by the movement and sober gestures of the characters more than by the limited phrases they exchange. These are not actors who speak to the public, they are beings capable of communicating in silence with each other, individuals that for reasons beyond themselves have suffered the gradual loss of their assets and are sharing a collective experience. At the very least they want to preserve their dignity and humbly try to hide the evidence of their misfortune. With moving subtlety, Ford reaches the depth of their feelings and makes us participate in this discovery. We identify with Tom Joad, who in the end leaves alone, without those who love him being able to do anything to help him. Disappointed, as we follow him to his exile, we notice that the peddlers of charity and proletarian unity–if we ever believed in them–can only be found when they need us and not when the establishment and the world appears to have turned against us. This is not a movie that will lift anyone's spirits. John Ford's proverbial optimism does not appear anywhere in this film. To give it a happy ending would have signified the triumph of collectivism over free initiative, and Ford believes in the individual overcoming his misfortunes by his own volition.

How Green Was My Valley - 1941

> Huw Morgan remembers his infancy, the death of
> his father, his sister's sacrifice, and the self-denial
> of his mother in the Welsh valley where he was
> born. He describes the economic and social
> changes that forced the break up of a family that
> was struggling to stay together.

The story takes place in a mining town, during the first part of the twentieth century, which someone describes to us based on his childhood memories. It is a fragmented story, where only the events that left an impression in the mind of that child are shown. He sees how his family, the strongest defense in his environment, begins to disintegrate for reasons beyond the wishes of every family member. The events are shown to us incomplete, with large gaps, as if nothing else happened in that valley in South Wales other than what is being narrated to us. In a reverie suited to his age, Huw transmits the images and events that most impressed him, magnified by time. The film is a family account given by a child, and it is also the perceptive revelation of the director of the movie, who—with astounding intuition—enters the mind of the narrator. It is a surprising breakdown of personalities that, in literature, is best illustrated by Dostoyevsky. The absence of the narrator in the recounting of his memories allows the director certain liberties with the story and frees him from having to offer additional explanations that in another situation would have been obligatory. This might be the most pessimistic film made by John Ford for anyone who believes that the deepest human feelings develop within the family context. The narrator remembers with tenderness the happy moments of the past while at the same time he makes a painful recollection of his anguish at the loss of those he most needed. I don't know if Hemmingway was quoting Pio Baroja when he said 'all history, in order to appear true, must always end in death.' This movie confirms that there is something true to this questionable statement.

An adult Huw Morgan—who does not appear onscreen—tells how he grew up and describes the circumstances that formed him while his family was destroyed. Ford picks up the story just as the child perceived it and narrates it as a distant memory of childhood. In a later film, *The Searchers*, he will effect a reverse transmutation–instead of Ford following the memories of a character, it will be the protagonist who will represent and execute the ideology of the author. In spite of *How Green Was My Valley* being the biography of a child, the film reaches out to even the most intellectually developed viewers. Ford doesn't want to make the story into an inconsequential drama, and in remembering the past, he finds our origins and explores the causes of the immigrations to America, describing their circumstances and trying to explain some of the reasons. He presents the moment and the setting that influenced the decision of the future immigrant, almost always under duress, and frequently in defense of their dignity. Through the voice of the new American we have the opportunity to examine the nature of the social conflict that developed in Europe during the first part of the last century. Confident in his own experience, he suggests that resistance to injustice more often comes from the resolution of the individual than from a collective effort driven by a demagogue.

In the higher levels of society, the variable phases of the economy have the effect of greater opulence or insecurity, according to which side of the balance sheet each magnate is located during the course of these fluctuations. For those who depend on daily work, these same economic events translate into well-being or misery, secure work or unemployment. An anthropologist might reach the conclusion that the notion of poverty has many subjective aspects, each with a different significance in the time and society in which they take place. This observer of human behavior could classify destitution as an abstraction that requires being comparatively examined. Its consequences, however, are wholly concrete, as it is for the person who experiences the pain of seeing the suffering, distancing of loved ones, or the dejection brought about by going to bed with an empty stomach. For someone to feel these overwhelming sensations mentioned, there is no need to make comparisons. Huw participates in these experiences early on and immediately realizes their destructive effects.

The minds of children, when exposed to the traumatic conditions of society, acquire a surprising precociousness. What the intellect of a child developing inside an environment of social struggle can perceive is incomprehensible to another whose family enjoys economic tranquility. The religious and political conflicts that reach the Morgans have a clear significance for Huw; he then realizes that the situation imposes certain restrictions on his family that are not possible to ignore. He manages to understand, inside his budding intellect, that the economy essentially depends on the worker, and that at the same time the worker must submit to the inevitable demands of production. He also learns early on that Christianity has two faces and two different interpretations in disagreement. From his earliest years, he recognizes woman as the supreme symbol of authority and discovers the matriarchal organization in an ancient culture of pre-Christian origin. During the movie, John Ford puts particular emphasis on these symbols that condition the thinking of the young Morgan, and which he will later summon with intense emotion. The experiences that

influenced the judgment and formation of Huw are represented through his memories during the most emotional moments of the film. There is an almost biblical scene, where the finger of the religious accuser covers most of the screen, concealing the faces of all of the parishioners. Afterwards, in opposition to the intolerance of that wretched and lecherous cleric, Mr. Gruffydd gives an emotional sermon against the hypocrisy that exists in the community. Another significant moment is when the mother emerges as the only force capable of imposing her will when the stature of the male is no longer respected.

Years later, Huw Morgan will discover that the habit of defending personal interest is present with similar intensity in all individuals. It is a substantial part in the evolution of each species, just like feeding off of others in order to survive. Trying to resist the consequences of a law of nature is like pretending to ignore the effects of gravity on our universe. This is the fate of the human being and his actions. John Ford considers man with benevolence as long as he remains faithful to his principles. He looks upon man with scorn when he behaves in an underhanded way; taking advantage of others in their misfortune. Two opposing forces and an intrusive opportunist represent the dramatic battle for existence in the world of Ford. They are like two solid columns with a third feeble appendage that merely gives balance to the structure. This last extremity is the shadow that highlights the splendor of the ideals and, by contrast, contributes to emphasizing the value of the struggle. Just as an object acquires greater stability when it rests on three points, drama achieves a better balance when it is based on elements that comprise a trilogy, although each is of a different value.

The humanist convictions of the director of *The Grapes of Wrath*–which will appear in later films–are confirmed in this film, in the face of the governing political theories of that time. If the tribulations that humanity experiences have a theological origin or their solutions are conformed to social theorists, literature would be finished–and more than likely so would any other possibility for art. Like all honest narrators and true philosophers, Ford does not promise solutions, he only presents the nature of the conflict and offers it for our consideration. He observes man as a part of nature, not detached from it, nor does he try to place him above his human condition. He also does not try to arrange the events in the interest of any particular tendencies. This impartiality of Ford is particularly irritating to those who claim to know the causes that provoke the battles between men. The conclusion that comes closest to the observations made in *How Green Was My Valley* is that human beings and their misfortunes, along with the rest of the species, follow the compass of chance. There are generous people capable of sacrificing themselves for others without expecting any reward. However, some take advantage of the tragedy of others and get more satisfaction from dwelling in the darker corners of their own existence. Nature, indifferent to moral issues, will not reward some and punish others. Within the melancholy that generally permeates this film, there is a trace of optimism. Just as in the better American literature of that time, it is character that makes the difference, much more than the context. Not only in literature, but during the politics of the first half of the twentieth century as well: Joe McCarthy was not defeated by his ideological enemies but by discreet and scrupulous gentlemen who rejected the inquisitorial methods used by the senator. What John Ford suggests is that the ethical conditions of an individual are not determined by either his religious beliefs or his economic status, but by the depth of his convictions, whatever they may be. The film develops according to what our experience has shown us about life: It is inevitable that some people will do better than others, and the struggle for life is also unavoidable. What is important is to always rise to the level of the circumstances and face the battle with dignity and determination.

They Were Expendable – 1945

In the Philippine Islands an American squadron is
abandoned and destroyed by the enemy when the
Second World War was about to end.

This film drifts through my memory as a protest against the humanist disguise
with which the sinister effects of war is embellished. Although I haven't had a
chance to see the movie a second time, my impression is it has a pacifist feeling in
the storyline. The intention of its creator is clear and summarized in the title. A
group of top American soldiers are abandoned for strategic reasons on a remote
island of the Pacific. The tactical needs of the moment require this military
detachment be left behind in order to avoid sacrificing many more. We already
knew that war was a dangerous game of execution and survival, but cinema had
not yet posed the possibility that it might also be a question of mathematics. What
is reported in a war is an insignificant portion of what those who experience it go
through. Under military command, objectives must be defended at whatever the
cost, and it doesn't matter how many innocent victims are sacrificed during the
conflict. In war's ominous shadow, crimes are committed that are impossible to
conceive under any other circumstances. Behind the advertised humanitarian
activities of armies lies their true destructive function, and a soldier is trained to
survive and kill at the same time–without any consideration for the human
condition of whoever occupies the enemy trenches. Afterwards, when troops are
also unable to guard prisoners during a march across hostile territories, they
sometimes must get rid of them. There is no escaping war; once it has started we
all become participants whether we want to or not. Everyone is affected, directly
or indirectly, and the future of each of us will be altered. Sometimes armed battle
is presented to us as an inevitable outcome, but we will never know for sure if
there was some other solution to the conflict. I don't know why, but the memory
of *They Were Expendable* brings to mind these reflections, like an involuntary and
fortuitous childhood memory.

During the past hundred years, the turbulence of war has yielded millions of cadavers across the entire world, but it must be recognized that the conscience of the past century has also left testimony of its desire for peace. The generations that saw some of the bloodiest conflicts that humanity has ever unleashed revealed a pacifist disposition in all cultural levels. From Tolstoy to "Guernica," from popular music to Hemingway, the condemnation of violence has been spontaneous and uncompromising, though almost always through statements dedicated to blaming the adversary. Nonetheless, the open declaration of pacifism is not the same as an assertion of innocence. Every political sector, each individual member of a party, contributes daily to the promotion of peace or violence. It is a fact that greater powers have greater responsibility, but we are all guilty to some degree. We seek to secure by any means necessary that which we believe is owed to us or that which we desire to possess. We dig trenches to defend our lives or graves to collect our bodies: "Do not ask for whom the bells toll," John Donne replies. *They Were Expendable* is a revealing episode of the cold calculations the military must make while carrying out its mission, and an example of the predicament that an army might occasionally face in order to fight effectively. The dilemma this film presents is part of the drama experienced by the war generations anywhere on Earth: Sacrificing some so that the rest can continue to live.

Ford's subtle indictment against the unavoidable barbarity of war has nothing to do with the ostentatious antiwar display the opportunistic and less sentient sector of the film industry indulges. Cinema and its producers are ambivalent about war. The industry is in favor of peace while at the same time it continues to prosper with its fictional violence. Hollywood, today the world capital of pacifism, is also the kingdom of superficiality. Confrontational at the start of its existence, it has become an irresponsible pacifist during the latter part of the previous century. Studios survive by the cultivation of make-believe violence, but those who labor within them pretend not to notice. Stars don't have to think too much to declare themselves against war rather than to search for the real cause for the violence unleashed by human beings. Actors and actresses dazzle only because they are stars–an external and transitory condition–which is why they feel the pressing need to feign interest in serious and transcendental issues. They live off the admiration of the greater segment of the public and do not want to do anything to diminish their popularity. Their declarations against war only serve to make evident the opportunism that drives them. Few have ever been tempted to go beyond the surface of ideas, but in spite of that, the opinions disseminated by this seemingly happy community are widely circulated. Influenced by the attention they receive, they do not want to discuss the contradiction between their positions in favor of peace and their mad dash towards success. In the product they help elaborate, characters only need to pretend and materials only need to appear to be real, so their fan base is already conditioned to accept superficialities. In any event, the prestige of the capital of cinema has always been justified by the group of privileged artists who have given it life and the legion of consummate professionals that make cinematic production possible. It is easier to find consequential and reflective individuals among this latter creative element.

John Ford's pacifism isn't casual. It is that of a man conscious that the violent condition of the human being is an integral part of nature. During the last world war, as a citizen he actively joined with his country in the war that America was carrying out on two continents. In *They Were Expendable* he makes a call to acknowledge the cold and brutal disposition of war, so distant from the apparatus destined to triumph in the name of justice that governments attribute to each conflict, to justify the sacrifice of the people. To proclaim oneself against war no longer has much significance, since there are few who do not do so, even those who generate a favorable atmosphere for it. Reflecting upon its causes and trying to find a peaceful solution to our differences is quite another. War, as Ford suggests, once unleashed leaves us no way out–passively or actively–we are all participants. His profound humanistic convictions would lead him to film this movie, which is nearly a declaration of principles and a condemnation against the interests that legitimize war. Violence is a part of the natural behavior that all species are forced to practice for their own survival. We must be aware of this because when the beast is unleashed, all we have to oppose it is some degree of civilization and the romantic spirit that might be inside each of us.

My Darling Clementine – 1946

In Tombstone, the youngest of the Earp brothers is
assassinated by Billy Clanton. Sheriff Wyatt Earp
gets to know Clementine Carter and engages in
friendly differences with an already ailing Doc
Holliday. Wyatt and Morgan Earp slay the Clanton
family at the O.K. Corral with the help of Doc
Holliday, who dies in the clash. Wyatt sees
Clementine leave.

The theme comes from a first-hand tale that passes into history thanks to the life
given to it by this movie. This film is a piece of the past and a feat of imagination
at the same time. John Ford was a passionate chronicler of periods of agony–times
that we know are gone forever but that we struggle to keep alive. This movie is a
glorious example of his passion for creating an intimate outline of history and
capturing the final accounts of a specific way of life. At the O.K. Corral, the
legendary Wild West makes its final mark before becoming more urbane and, like
Wyatt Earp, moves to Hollywood to spend eternity in the Paradise of Dreams.
Before its departure, through a drunk and nomadic actor, Tombstone and Hamlet
begin a strange and frustrated coexistence in the form of Doc Holliday, the all-
male Clanton family, and the sheriff. The two female characters in this movie
(Chihuahua and Clementine)–the only hope of the antagonists had they
survived–appear as the symbol of a refuge that was never accepted. When Ford
photographed the sequences of this movie, another ending could be glimpsed in
the cinematographical horizon: The gradual departure of black-and-white films
from the landscape.

Color began its domination in 1946, and the importance of its tones was valued
with the same interest in which the general public discussed the overall quality of
a film. By then, John Ford had already filmed a few movies with the new
technology and knew from experience the advantages and limitations of both
techniques. For the images of this new cinema to compete with the fascination that
Technicolor exerted on the public was a challenge that he confronted by

accentuating that which color could offer no advantage in traditional photography: contrasts. In *My Darling Clementine* Ford dispenses with the fog and the half-tones while using the light of the desert to illuminate the ambience, shifting it all the way into the interior scenes. The photographic details are even more pronounced this time and Arizona's luminosity contributes with its dawns and twilight to prolong the shadows and bring emphasis to the contrasts. As Françoise Truffaut said, "Ford was an artist who did not like to talk about art and a poet who never spoke of poetry."

Even though *My Darling Clementine* takes place in a violent environment, the movie is a prelude to a secret love that remains hidden, not only from the rest of the characters in the film but also from the viewer. This platonic feeling of Wyatt Earp, like the unbridled passion of Chihuahua or the self-sacrificing disposition of Clementine, remain frustrated, without even the slightest possibility of culminating in a happy conclusion. In spite of the frustration that overwhelms the characters, a romantic symbolism prevails throughout the narration, giving the film a deep sentimental significance, even when the spectator is confronted with the more violent sequences. By representing the feminine image in an environment of struggle and uncertainty, the film brings to mind the much more savage characteristics the conquest of the American West must have had during those episodes in which woman was not present to keep check the males' impetuous fury. The director further illustrates this by delving into a community in the process of formation, where woman is the only one capable in some measure to mitigate the aggressive behavior of man. As usual with Ford, simple and without big gestures, he illustrates the relevance of a transcendental sociological event–this time in the accessible and apt setting of the American West. While he profiles the characteristics of the inhabitants of Tombstone, he invites us to reflect on a not-so-distant past and poetically represents the manner in which America's civic heritage has since been determined by the presence of woman. The director didn't allow his fantasy to forget this reality, and even though the violent scenes were the ones that got the most attention from the public, the higher significance of this film corresponds to the femininity, which might be why this movie is named after a woman.

Maternity in its various stages has been a constant point of reference in Ford cinema. In *How Green Was My Valley* or *The Grapes of Wrath* the woman is the solid pillar behind which the family unites to face adversity. In another film, the most diverse human specimens assist a birth that takes place under difficult circumstances, and is the only moment in which all the travelers of *Stagecoach* have something in common to celebrate. The decisive manner in which the heroes of Ford cinema conduct themselves revolves reverently around the woman and become humble and sympathetic toward the image that mother represents. *My Darling Clementine* is a violent statement in favor of matriarchy, without which–it tells us–confrontation is inevitable and devastating. The cosmology of the author proclaims his European background and Christian origin. Ford does not forget the cross, which appears repeatedly and on significant occasions. The cross and motherhood are the two ingredients that Europe contributes to extend religion and to soften the divine rage announced in the Bible. Avoiding all religious ceremonies, Ford does not allow providence or even luck to interfere in favor of either of the two parts in conflict. Rationalism imposes its norms during the film and allows a deeply rooted paganism to be seen in the subconscious of the characters.

In the series of preconceived scenes of any narrator, there are usually situations that sometimes transcend the needs of the story, which might be added in later. Just as in other artistic fields, by means of a secret mechanism of some sort, the mind of the film director inserts sequences into a movie. Their effect will often be actualized during filming or editing. These intuitive, fleeting revelations are like unintentional discoveries made by the creator's subconscious–something that in a particular instant springs unexpectedly from his mind and will not happen again the same way on any other occasion. This is how, through an unknown process, time integrates itself to the work and contributes to make it unique: A melody, a thought, or a brushstroke respond to the impulse of the mind and is also a consequence of the instant in which it was executed. Had it taken place in another time, the musical note would not have surged from the same emotional state of the composer and would be different. The mind of the poet will not be of the same disposition to perceive the idea a day later, nor will it find the same inspiration as the impetus to compose the sonnet conceived in a moment of passion or melancholy. The painter's palette will not have the same mixture of colors in any other instant and these colors will not affect his retina in the same way, nor will his brushstroke be applied with identical intensity or extension at any other hour of the day. More than style, it is those uncontrollable impulses that surge from the subconscious of the artist that will give his work a personal and distinctive character. Instantaneous reactions are transmitted to the sensibility of the viewer, who might decide to reflect on their mysterious origin and as an inevitable consequence, try to understand the mind of the one who gave them significance.

The episode at the O.K. Corral was already a part of the legend of the American West before *My Darling Clementine*. Let's talk a bit about what is known of the character of the individuals involved: Doc Holliday, inveterate player ill with the effects of a plague that lashed humanity during several decades. (If he were alive today he would be in good health in Las Vegas.) Even back then his presence in Tombstone does not appear very probable. Apparently the Earp brothers arrived in Tombstone from Dodge City, a city that, according to the chroniclers of the time, had one of the worst reputations in the United States. This seems to point to the reality that they did not possess the altruistic civic disposition attributed to them in the film. What is known about their activities up to then is that they were very close to criminal and had likely taken place mostly outside the law. It doesn't make any sense for the Clantons to decide to provoke these dangerous outsiders. It is quite possible that the Earps' arrival in Tombstone might have had different intentions from those given in the film. Wyatt, the elder brother, was not recognized as a rancher but as one of the more able gunmen circulating the American plains. On the other hand, as far as we know the Clantons were ranchers in Arizona, possibly forming part of that community for many years. The peaceful disposition conceded to the Clantons by certain meticulous historians is in step with their stable position within the community. It is difficult to believe that within this panorama they would have been the ones trying to divest the Earps of their livestock. All of these circumstances, as well as the questionable past of the sheriff, come into conflict with the film director's intentions: Ford undoubtedly wanted to create his own version of reality. Without worrying about what might have happened historically and to give life to the product of his imagination, Ford invents a setting where the resulting situation is more realistic and convincing in the opinion of the viewer. In the movie, the representation made by the director must be unquestionably logical, and, consequently, even more acceptable to the public than the capricious or nonsensical course of life.

That which serves to stimulate the imagination of the artist, enrich his fantasy, and ultimately establish an intense communication with the public is what the work of any genre must be intended to transmit. The customary payment of royalties releases producers who might have creative intentions from having to adhere to the text of the novel. In this manner the director does not have to worry about criticism from those who expect to see the reproduction of history or a literary work in a film. John Ford has freely exercised the freedom given by the public to artistic fantasy and makes it count in each of his movies. By adjusting the historical text to the needs of his imagination in *Mary of Scotland*, he reduces the transcendental religious conflict that changes the destiny of an empire to the clash between two women of opposing character and temperament. In *The Informer* he transforms a novel by Liam O'Flaherty about Ireland's struggle for independence into a psychological observation of a drunken man with no future during the last night of his life. There might be those who think that he should follow the text or that he frequently takes too much advantage of the liberties conceded to film. It actually seems that John Ford never really allowed himself another alternative, except to follow the inclinations demanded by his own inspiration. Whatever the origin and nature of the dispute between the

Clanton family and the Earp brothers in real life, it is certain that prior to beginning the film, Ford was already planning on changing the story. It is evident that the director wanted the actual events he was planning on telling to only serve the needs of his work. The reasons that brought about the duel in the O.K. Corral might have been different from those presented by the author of the film. Although not necessarily opposites, imagination and reality are indeed different. The latter was the starting point of the story, while the other helped develop the drama and give it meaning. To faithfully reflect history would not have been of any use to the director's purposes. By altering it he was able to realize one of the most brilliant works in cinematography.

Two groups of brothers, beyond the reach of the cautious and consoling maternal advice, confront each other. The different ways this circumstance affects each of these families lies in that the Clantons–for reasons not apparent in the movie–appear to be indifferent to the absence of woman within their family composition, and they do not realize the significance of this factor in their behavior. Anything that might elevate the civic level of the population is alien to them. The moving verses that a dipsomaniac actor and Doc Holliday recite appear to sound insulting to the Clantons' ears. In contrast, the Earps conduct themselves in a more civilized manner, evident in their integration into the community and the respect they show for a society represented by the female image. In spite of being recent arrivals, they are buoyed by a solidarity with the families of their new neighbors and demonstrate it in the conflict that is sparked when a woman from the town is assassinated. The friendly reception by the inhabitants of Tombstone encourages the Earps to conduct themselves within the law and become responsible for the security of the town. Quite unlike the prudent disposition of the Earps, the Clanton brothers and their father do not have any bonds that join them to anyone else, and they act certain of not having to respond to anyone for anything. Full of fury, they defy the others without a preconceived strategy, counting only on their weapons and resolution. On the other side, the battle plan designed by Wyatt is done so with meticulous care to every tactical detail, just as the men who will join him calmly and methodically prepare for the challenge. They go to the O.K. Corral believing in their mission, and while only one of the members of the sheriff's squad marches to the battle without hope, the rest hope to survive to become part of the future of Tombstone.

Without even thinking about it, John Ford has the circumstances explain and give strength to the story, bringing it to us with utmost intensity. This ability flows unconsciously from his creative instinct. Things could have happened differently, but to those characters he created and in the environment that he reproduced, everything had to happen to them in the manner in which he tells us. The behavior of the Clanton brothers is only conceivable when taking into consideration their motherless background. The fatherly whip punishes while also serving as the instrument for the education and handling of his offspring, but it is a poor substitute for the solace a feminine presence could have given them. Without a maternal guide, like injured wolves, old man Clanton and his sons wander across the screen toward their extinction. They are the inevitable victims of this drama, which has woman on one end and the lack of her at the other. The dance of the pioneer families in front of the unfinished church has a promising significance and points to a hopeful future. On the other end, everything was desolate and without a future. On a more tangible level, Ford presents us two masterfully defined facets of woman, as personified by the exquisite and civilized Clementine and the savage and earthy Chihuahua. The pain that the death of the latter produces in us reminds us that she, too, had contributed something to the life of Tombstone and that the town had a place for her in its future. Doc Holliday is like an anecdotal character: Somewhat stiff, almost superfluous, sort of like the first tourist in the desert. He serves only to draw Clementine to Arizona and introduce her image into the movie.

Death is the main protagonist of this film. It is introduced to us shortly after the start of the movie and ends with the desperate gesture of old man Clanton, a mixture of execution and suicide. This is a moment of enormous psychological weight: Clanton leaves his hideout fearful, but also happy to be alive. He begins walking toward freedom when suddenly, once he is safe, he decides life isn't worth living anymore. Where does this sudden change take place? In the mind of the movie director? No, John Ford senses it in the mind of Clanton. Like a Herodotus of film, he recounts the episode not too far from where it took place and very close to when it happened. As each of the characters disappears, it produces a sensation of distress that reaches out to us from the screen. We see how they fall one by one, brought down by circumstances rather than their own fault, leaving in us the painful sensation of an inevitable outcome. All death has a terrible significance, but only for the contemporaries of the dead. In retrospect, five or fifty years later it is merely something that had to happen, because the dead belong to a time that has passed. In the same way the force of gravity diminishes as bodies move away from each other. A tragic event pains us in inverse proportion to the time that has past. Otherwise, we wouldn't be able to endure the anguish created by the accumulated pain, and our planet would only be populated by soulless beings. Re-creating the past, making us feel as if it were the present and to have this new reality enlighten our spirit is the work of a genius. With magical dexterity, Ford transports us to a time and place that his imagination has created for us. He makes Tombstone come alive before our eyes, and we can feel in all its intensity the life and death of those pioneers who traversed the deserts of Arizona in a brief moment of history.

TF-Pub-1465

The Fugitive – 1946

Following the triumph of the Mexican Revolution,
a priest is forced to escape and finds refuge in a
distant and impoverished area of Mexico. In the
end he is captured and executed.

Each character in this narrative is a symbol. So that there is no doubt about
this, they lack names and their images do not correspond to their personal
identities. All are a representation of some culture and personify a specific
activity or trade. The doctor, the organ grinder, and the policeman are
prototypes of their respective professions. The Indian woman and the gringo
signify two different appreciations of the same situation. The fugitive is a
cleric full of doubts, a priest who isn't very certain of the effectiveness of
his apostolic mission. His tribulations are only anecdotes that serve to
emphasize the essential struggle the preist has with his conscience. After his
escape, he has had the opportunity to appreciate the way that indigenous
customs affect the interpretation of the doctrine he shares with them. At the
same time, as a spectator the priest begins to realize that moral concepts
differ within each culture, and he sees how these have changed over time.
The society that welcomes the fugitive is based on a pantheist foundation
that Christianity has not completely dissolved. Their primitive gods behave
in a capricious manner, are less almighty, and more in agreement with the
laws of nature. In contrast to Middle Eastern Messianism, these pagan
symbols do not have the pretension of giving answers to the moral conflicts
that man must resolve on his own. The cleric recognizes the brutal trauma
suffered by these indigenous people when they were forced to submit their
customs to the dictates of his faith. He finds out how that cruel experience
left a deep impression on the idiosyncrasies of those towns. Conversion to
the Christian doctrine was not the compassionate and civilizing action we
have been led to believe, but an imposition by force. The conquest of
America by the Spanish was reminiscent of the Muslim invasion suffered by
the Iberian Peninsula eight hundred years earlier. The same religious
fanaticism that encouraged the warrior determination of the Arabian people

inspired Spain's colonizing purposes in the New Continent. The methods employed by both conquests are so similar that, exchanging the cross for the half moon, it is difficult to distinguish any differences in the purposes and procedures of either invasion. Shortly after the Spanish conquest, the Arabian influence that Spain had introduced within its Christianity would be felt in Europe and in the New Continent by means of the Inquisition.

A culture's past has ramifications in the social behavior of an individual and a people; the religiousness of the fugitive is influenced by that which he has inherited from the pre-Christian culture and the Christianity of the natives by the atavistic beliefs of their ancestors. The fugitive priest understands that these indigenous villages have come to Catholicism through a completely different path than his. They participate in the same religion, but their interpretation is conditioned by other customs. Pagan traces that affect the subconscious are hidden in the past of the civilization to which the priest now belongs. These circumstances facilitate the solidarity of the fugitive with the village that harbors him. Fifteen hundred years earlier the worship of nature's majesty practiced by Europeans suffered a similar dispossession. Europe was also forced to renounce their merry gods and submit a joyous ancestral culture to the pathetic cult of the bible. Even though it happened at different times and with different consequences to each, the two civilizations suffered the effects of the gradual loss of their culture and identity by the same religious conspiracy. Previously, on the other side of the Atlantic, religion had brought about equally painful results to a different and more evolved society. His European cultural inheritance, born from the conflict between rationality and divinity, allows the fugitive to identify with the natives and awakes doubts as to the generosity and tolerance of Christianity. The big difference of both paganisms with respect to religion is that in the pantheistic mythology no one is forced to believe, nor are there any attempts at deceit, as found in the articles of faith.

With the arrival of Christianity, the ancient continent succumbed to sophism and abandoned the mythological heroes of its millennial polytheism. These irreverent gods became metaphoric figures used to illustrate ideas, entertain the imagination, and adorn spaces. All of this without meddling with the private lives of human beings. Different from the almighty God, the European deities did not know how to write and let man examine his conscience on his own. This open disposition with regards to the mind made philosophical debate possible and from that classical period to our time has facilitated free analysis, moral discussions, and the development of ethics. Those of us who have inherited that culture are willing to sacrifice ourselves to maintain honor rather than pay tribute to the glory of a supernatural being. In comparison, the written word of the Oriental god ominously demands submission and rejects regulating our conduct according to reason and logic. Even worse, its descendents want to force us to recognize the existence of wisdom within its undignified behavior. In spite of the glorious superiority of Greco-Roman thinking, the intrusive monotheistic scripture is established as absolute truth, disavows the feats of mythological characters, and condemns them. Those who rejected the creative European tradition, the Mosaics, Christians, and Mohammedans–the three messianic sects that adjust their morals to ineffective and arbitrary commandments–accept as their religious role model the same filicidal and abject patriarch. The princes of sophism adorn their lies with virtuous and devout rules. When man refuses to recognize his own ignorance with the purpose of pretending wisdom, he invents an Almighty God to give explanation to the unknown. He personifies decadence–arrogantly, he feels destined to create the supernatural, thereby losing Greece and, without knowing it, closing the doors on true paradise. The film doesn't directly approach these types of considerations, but the protagonist and his surroundings are clearly affected by the past of these respective historical experiences. What for Graham Greene is a religious subject is for Ford a topic of speculation, a cinematic allegory that hardly borrows from literature.

It might be possible to reconcile the limitations the critics attributed to this story with the opinion John Ford had of his movie. What the spectator will find lacking in this film is the director's connection to the drama in the original novel. There is a noticeable difference between the Christianity of John Ford and the Catholic fervor professed by the rural class in Mexico, and this appears to limit his ability to deeply comprehend their faith. The rational disposition of the director and the geographical proximity of that country did not help him to sufficiently penetrate the mind of the indigenous culture, and this circumstance results in the lack of the most inspiring element of his cinema: passion. Ford can identify with the conflict that develops in the conscience of the leading protagonist, but appears to also have been aware of the distance that separates him from the rest of the characters. With the exception of the fugitive, all the other symbols belong to a distant world that Ford can only observe from afar. It is not possible to have intimate contact with those who react to different impulses, and it is also more difficult to identify with their feelings. This film lacks intensity because the director's deep understanding of the drama experienced by the peasants is missing. Passion is not something that relies on will, not even exclusively on the temperament of the director, but in some measure it is also based on the context. *The Informer* is essentially a film that concentrates on a single person, but during the progression of the narrative, the director begins to intimately identify with even the most insignificant character of this Irish tale. The reverse happens in *The Fugitive*, where he remains outside of the movie like a demanding and detached critic who must only observe with no reason to interfere. The psychological distance that separates the director from the characters he portrays in this movie filmed in Mexico had, without a doubt, something to do with the results. For different reasons, in *Mary of Scotland* there is a similar disconnect by John Ford with respect to the historical figures represented and, although this movie enjoyed great success, it also is not one of his best films. Let's continue speculating: Maybe the religious subject was an obstacle to the director's interpretation of the characters, but perhaps someone else knows of another barrier preventing John Ford from becoming more intensely involved in the situations he was describing.

Ford had never before tackled a purely religious theme. From what can be observed through his films, religion to him was not a dominant subject but a question of tradition and faith that should not interfere at all in the rationality of a work. His particular religious bond was not something destined to diminish the open and expressionistic realism of his cinema. The story of *The Fugitive* appears to be narrated by an ethics professor who explains the episode in detail, but is also indifferent to the events. Ford's absence is felt during the movie, and the passionate defense that he usually makes for the fundamental ethics of our culture is missing. The identification with the story that he manages in his other movies does not take place on this occasion and, consequently, the viewer only manages to be a distant observer. Innumerable defects have been ascribed to this film, which Ford held in great esteem, among them that the director was not more faithful to the novel that gave him the original idea. This is a banal accusation. The greater the freedom in developing a movie, the greater the possibilities are for a creative work. Apparently the reactions of some critics were the consequence of the film not responding to the expectations of action so often found in the movies of Ford, but the director's objective might have been quite different this time. It is obvious in this film that Ford was striving to produce a less dynamic sensation in the viewer and a

more moving and suggestive one with the scenes. Perhaps seduced by the indigenous magic of the country where this story was filmed, the director wished to leave a visual testimonial of his experience. In this sense the movie is sensational. The outlines of the figures against the indistinct background give the images an incomparable expressive force. Some of the sequences are of such beauty that they are fascinating. Perhaps the purpose of making this movie was purely expressionist, and it is possible that his perspective was conditioned by the plastic merit of photography. With the help of Gabriel Figueroa, he composed some of the most captivating images and obtained visual effects of a profound force ahead of their time. In spite of the limitations attributed, this movie is one of the most notable examples of cinematic realism. Each scene of the film is on its own a work of art that deserves to be contemplated several times.

Even though he qualified it as perfect, to many this was not one of John Ford's best films. To some, the director's declarations in favor of this movie were disconcerting, and to his followers, they continue to be a subject of curiosity. If he thought that this drama–filmed in the country where the story takes place–was outstanding, it must have been for a reason upon which he didn't care to share. As he never explained his preferences, one can speculate on the qualities he might have seen in the result of his work. To be fair, we must accept the possibility that there is justification in the contradictory perceptions of the critics and the director. The most notable is that the filming of these scenes took place immediately after *My Darling Clementine*, one of his most inspired masterworks. Even though both films have many similarities in the expressive intentions of their images, nobody would suspect that these two movies were conceived by the same person. Ford said he enjoyed *The Fugitive* every time he saw it. This statement, made many years later, suggests the possibility that he compared the film to movies of other directors. The pleasure of watching *The Fugitive* could be the result of having seen *La Strada* or *The Seven Samurai* and realizing that these wonderful films have a notable visual similarity to his. It is possible that the expressionistic intention of the Japanese film and the realism of the Italian movie might seem related to *The Fugitive* and generated in him the great satisfaction he asserted. This hypothesis does not explain Ford's preference, but it might explain his benevolent disposition towards a drama that perhaps some were never able to understand very well. As he never gave the reasons for his preference, it is only fair to speculate on what they might have been. But to be just, we must accept that there might be validity in both perceptions of the critics and the director. It is worthwhile to consider John Ford's criteria, because within the efforts of the great masters there are always some virtues to be found that will be invisible to the inept observer. For example, *Ginger and Fred* by Federico Fellini, a movie that was severely attacked by the critics, is more imaginative and poetic than most of the successful movies made since then. In this nostalgic story by the Italian director, it is evident that even the most minimal work of a genius is above the criticism of the mediocre. In spite of any existing deficiencies, *The Fugitive* is an impressive spectacle of images, symbols, and sacrilege.

Fort Apache – 1948
She Wore a Yellow Ribbon – 1949
Rio Grande – 1950

Colonel Owen Thursday begins a disastrous campaign against the Apaches. Captain Kirby York later corrects the mistakes of the colonel and convinces the Indians to return to the reservation, promising the respect and protection of the Army. Philadelphia Thursday, daughter of Owen, marries the son of the sergeant, and the factions of the cavalry are reconciled.

A journey through Monument Valley during the last mission of veteran Captain Brittles. The captain tackles skirmishes with the Indians after General Custer's defeat. The aging military man now relies on his experience to provide political solutions to conflicts.

After sixteen years, Captain Kirby York is reunited with his wife, Kathleen, and his son Jeff, who also serves in the cavalry. During a conflict with the Indians, the captain is injured and Jeff extracts the embedded arrow from his father's body.

This trilogy of the American cavalry is a ballad dedicated to the anonymous heroes who contributed to the creation of our country: "Professional soldiers for fifty cents a day." These movies are also important for they begin to give the western an ethnic focal point. That is to say, the cultural background performs a fundamental role in the conflicts between Indians and the white man. The Indian presence in the movie ceases to be simply anecdotal and becomes a sociological matter worthy of comment. The outcome of the conflict has been registered in favor of the recent arrivals, but the ethical panorama at issue clearly leans towards the rights of the defeated. The cinema of John Ford refuses to accept all the episodes of history as positives, and through the nonconformity of his characters he creates doubts of the justice of this unfortunate outcome. The final result is not important. Ford wants to bring the viewer's attention to the legitimacy of the Indians' fight against the white man.

Without an army's means at their disposal, the natives of the country tenaciously resist the conquest of a territory that, in their judgment, should be open to the passage of everyone. The deep conviction that they are respecting the wishes of nature justifies their skirmishes and feeds their hopes of victory. Their resistance is in defense of their way of life. They will fight as long as possible, just as the

mother will abandon her pup only when it is inevitable it will be devoured by the beast. Cultures will also flee the battle in the face of the inevitable tides of history. It was a question of conscience that would affect the thinking of the new American being born. From there the free man emerges, who founded his Home on the Land of the Brave and who has left the certainty of this experience engraved in a hymn. The past is a burden we all have to carry and which each of us is obligated to learn. History will teach us how to face the future and how to better affect it, but there is no reason to expect clemency from its implacable judgment.

These three films are built upon the same structure: The American cavalry has established positions in the outposts of the white settlements extending without a break to the West of the continent, and the soldiers have the duty of protecting the migrating colonies that are being established. The situation can be hostile, and patrolling the area implies frequent risks and facing unexpected dangers. The memory of Little Big Horn is still fresh, and the military is on permanent alert to prevent that sort of disaster from happening again. These are soldiers used to combat; many of them were recruited from either side of the Civil War, which ended a few years earlier. Disputes between the settlers and the Indians are

inevitable, as the territory in question has a different significance to each of these two cultures. The armored detachment of the western outpost was not conceived to serve as arbiter in these conflicts, but to protect the white man and extend its frontiers. They distinguish themselves as a military when they carry out their duties, and it is irrelevant to them if what they are doing is only witnessed by those who do not know the circumstance, nor the objectives of their mission. No army has ever been conceived to defend the rights of the adversaries. These horsemen are conscious that the future is being forged with the stride of their horses, and they have been entrusted to ensure that the defeat of General Custer does not represent a definitive victory for Sitting Bull. Nothing should change the course of the aspirations of the newcomer, who will infuse those regions with the norms of conduct to be followed by all who tread on that land under dispute. The cavalry is responsible for making sure nothing opposes this purpose or delays the conquest of these territories in the American West.

The landscape is the main show in these three movies. Ford moves around Monument Valley with a voluptuous insistence. The splendid scenery fits the epic appearance the director wants to give to his stories, but not everything takes place

outdoors. Within the forts where the soldiers are mobilized there is a life worthy of observation. To know them better, John Ford has decided to examine the behavior of the military in the two different environments: Within the security of the fort, and outside it, facing uncertainty and danger during their patrols. Characters appear and disappear in each of the three stories, while the director profiles them and portrays their fascinating world. The pragmatic and disciplined personality of Colonel Owen Thursday contrasts with the rash individuality of Captain Kirby York, and the sentimental stoicism of Kathleen York–who must share the love of her husband with his loyalty to the cavalry. The young, almost adolescent, Philadelphia Thursday is an innocent flower in a jungle of men. John Ford's favorite sergeant, Quincannon, is present every time the director wants to give a festive tone to the movie. Captain Nathan Brittles, a "courteous soldier and Christian gentleman"–having surveyed that valley from all points of the compass, in all types of weather and during all hours of the day–is filled with melancholy at his approaching retirement. The soldiers in these forts have diverse backgrounds and some of them have previously fought on opposing sides. They are now united in a common goal, and the offenses of the past are only an embarrassing memory. The respect they feel for each other is reflected in the discreet reverence with which the director shows these forgotten heroes. The exterior scenes the director filmed in Monument Valley are evidence of his unconscious pagan calling and a tribute to the imposing majesty of nature.

The Quiet Man – 1952

> Sean Thornton retires from boxing after killing his
> adversary in the ring and arrives in Ireland to
> distance himself from that event. In the small town
> of Innisfree he meets Kate Danaher and her
> brother, Red Will; he marries her and fights with
> him–a rite of passage that Sean doesn't understand
> but that the entire town celebrates.

An individual appears in Ireland after a tragic event, which is a cliché that could
have turned this movie into a melodrama, but the result is a comedy in the style of
movies of that time but with the flavor and originality of a Shakespearean sonnet.
The entire plot of the film revolves around this stranger who arrives with the
intention of staying in a place whose population is not used to visitors. As it
frequently happens in these situations, the new neighbor quickly becomes the
center of attention in the community. Everyone in Innisfree has known each other
for generations and conducts themselves according to what is expected from one
another. The lives of its inhabitants have gone on for years almost without change,
and no one's past is unknown. When there are no secrets in the past, these aged
societies develop an avid interest in the present, and that makes them more prone
to gossip. They accept the American's somewhat extravagant behavior, but they do
not tolerate a lack of information. Through a flashback we learn that Sean
Thornton conceals a tragic accident in his past, and naturally they all want to
share. This attitude of the foreigner, who refuses to satisfy people's expectations, is
interpreted by some as offensive, and they decide to dog his every step. His
discretion, more than anything else, sets him apart from the rest of the neighbors
and prevents him from socially integrating himself into the community. This is the
preface to the movie, and humor will be its unlimited resource for development.

We must believe in a story for it to have an effect on us. Ford places us in a
different setting, one that we might never have imagined, but we are instantly
convinced of its existence. The characters are so perfectly integrated into the
landscape, like the countenance of the actors to the demands of the script. When

the American of Irish origin arrives in Innisfree, he finds his ancestral home just as he had imagined it. He is in search of calm and oblivion, but finds something more exciting in Mary Kate Danaher. Her response to his interest encourages him to follow his impulses which eventually leads to matrimony. However, everything would have been much simpler somewhere else: Here the wish of the two lovers requires the approval of the community or at least of its more prominent members. The entire town wants to participate in some measure in this romance, and approval is given. All but one wishes to celebrate the impending culmination of the quiet romance. The brother of the bride, not the most respectable but certainly the most stubborn, harasses the suitor and tries to make life for the bride and groom impossible. Neither of the lovers is very young, but first she, then he, find an intoxicating pleasure in submitting to the traditional customs of the country, even if these are a bit intrusive. With unsurpassable humor Ford appears to suggest that love conquers all...as long as we conform to the demands imposed by society. The spirits of *The Taming of the Shrew* and *Much Ado About Nothing* appear to circle around the theater during the showing of this movie.

No other subject has been used as often in film as the emotional relationship between individuals of the opposite sex, from their meeting through the happy progress of their union. Just when we thought all possibilities had been exhausted, Ford surprises us with a fascinating realism, and quite different from what we have been exposed to previously. Starting with a rural community, John Ford exposes the lifestyle of its inhabitants and the peculiar formalities that must be adhered to prior to matrimony. He gathers the traditions of the country of his ancestors and describes a process that is almost ceremonial in which the genders must relate socially, influenced by a timeless pagan tradition that has been absorbed by Christianity. This is an ancient society with atavistic customs that are still in use in the more remote parts of Europe. This time, religion is represented by two clerics from different sects that intervene in everything that has to do with the life of the community and are in charge of polishing the souls of their citizens. The liberalism of the people is revealed through the festive character of the matchmaker, a somewhat irreverent and cynical character. With each image and every face, the attitude of every individual contributes to create the atmosphere of lively enthusiasm the director requires for the movie. The charm that this film brings to us prevents us from looking for a deeper meaning in the story, but when watching it on the screen, we experience a long-lasting sensation of having discovered a new paradise. This is an Irish movie made from an American perspective, or an American film constructed from an Irish point of view. Either way, only a man of both worlds could have conceived it.

Ford falls victim to captivating aesthetic impulses when undertaking the subject of Ireland. Undoubtedly this has added to the visual beauty of the film that can only be compared to the most lavish musical-comedy productions. With the frustrated desires of the main actress, he achieves a woman of incomparable femininity and seduction, while at the same time praising the virile and gentlemanly image of the suitor, who accedes to all the peculiar regional customs for her. Ford saturates the movie with scenic beauty and imbues the extensive repertory of gestures of the supporting actors with grace. These develop inside a festive ambiance that the arrival of the American visitor has produced in the bucolic calm of the town. The atmosphere suggests a romantic melody or a symphony in minor key, and its scenery has an appearance in keeping with movies of that time. Ford wasn't indifferent to the color and splendor of those movies, but the realism that his work demanded prevented him from following the somewhat limited path of those films. One can't interrupt the action to interject dreams that paralyze the storyline and diminish the expressive force of the characters. Nonetheless, *The Quiet Man* continues to have all the charm of musical films of the fifties. The endless fight between Sean Thornton and Red Will Danaher that goes on throughout the countryside is done with choreography reminiscent of *Seven Brides for Seven Brothers* or *West Side Story*. That was a more extroverted type of cinema that for obvious reasons Ford never tackled. His interest was more in the depth of the characters. The gestures and silences of the actors had more expressive value for the psychological aim he sought. This was the closest movie to a musical comedy that he made, a suggestive homage to his beloved Ireland. We can only imagine what would have been left of the deep and masterly portrayal of the characters in this story, if during a choreographic arrangement they had burst into song and dance. In art as in physics, what is gained in extension is lost in depth. Even so, in this film, as in the musical works of that time, fantasy wanders towards us from the screen, but here the director does not allow music to totally own the setting. Like a sentimental magician, with his camera Ford brings us to an idyllic emerald land, populated by muses and leprechauns.

Mister Roberts – 1955

During the Second World War, Lieutenant Howard
Roberts and the captain of a cargo ship in the
Pacific have some differences. The palm tree in
front of the captain's cabin that is twice hurled into
the ocean is a symbol of their disputes.

John Ford observes with particular interest a small segment of the Navy during its
moments of recreation and provides us with the circumstances in which they live
together. This wartime story defines characters that inspired the subject for film and
television for decades to come. Following *Mister Roberts*, many other movies took
advantage of the particular situations produced when military discipline prevents the
desire for freedom and expression that each person carries inside. Sitcoms destined to
be shown on television screens for years were inspired by the stimulating possibilities
for humor within military life that is revealed in this film. The field of activity of the
characters is limited to the interior and the deck of a cargo ship where the hours go
by slowly and nothing much appears to happen. The war in the Pacific was about to
end and from the bow of the ship, a group of Marines surveys the horizon in search
of entertainment. They see a hospital on the coast and the nurses get their attention.
The situations arising from this fortuitous encounter are inconsequential, but they
allow each of the sailors to show their idiosyncrasies and externalize their concerns.
This profound communication between them is what guides this film, which is like a
journey through the interior of the protagonists as well as a sentimental experience
born from the discoveries the sailors are making about themselves. The tedium
doesn't diminish the cheerful spirit of the crew, as the sailors are willing to find
diversions under any pretext. They are in festive spirits and share the optimism
brought by the proximity to the end of war. They exhibit a common disposition when
news is received, but as far as their conduct is concerned, Ford creates a human
profile that is quite distinct for each of them.

An impressive cast of actors was entrusted with representing these suggestive
personalities, whose days pass between sentimentality and idleness. When this
movie was released, color was already widely in use. Had it been filmed in black

and white a few years earlier, it is probable that the emotional exchange that takes place between the crew would have prevented this movie from being categorized as a comedy. The reading of the letter by Howard Roberts to his companions is so dramatic that it distances the mind of the viewer from any comedic sensation. It is as if the sailor's message was creating living images on the deck of that ship. Without being a proper comedy and aside from its moving ending, this film is one of the most inspired humorist works that has ever been shown onscreen. The casual style of story and jovial disposition of the protagonists of *Mister Roberts* can also be found in the occupants of the castles described by P.G. Wodehouse. It would be interesting to learn if, like Orson Welles, John Ford was also an assiduous reader of this British author's work. In spite of the story's melancholy tone, the humor shown by the American director in this and his other movies appears to be related to the irony with which the English novelist had been delighting his readers around the world for almost a century.

Without establishing a clear line of separation, classifications of the different genres in cinematography have been made in a fairly arbitrary way. Several tendencies entwine with each other in the same film, and it is difficult to precisely identify to which formula a particular movie belongs. Ingredients that are common to different genres are frequently found within the same movie, which is why sometimes it takes a bit of effort to separate the western from the drama or comedy. Without belonging to a particular cinematic tendency, humor is sometimes presented as the unconscious product of the director, without consideration to the text upon which the movie is based. The attempt a comedian frequently makes with respect to humor is the reason for the public's general tendency to consider comedy a synonym of humor, even though there should be no confusion in the meanings of these terms. Comedy has been designed for the public while humor is introspective and conceived to penetrate the conscience of certain people. Cinema has not contributed to clarify anything that might distinguish one from the other, because it is not an activity interested in establishing differences between the two notions. Assuming this could be of some importance, the reasons for this imprecision do not always originate with the decisions of the director but sometimes derive from the inaccurate meaning attributed by certain sectors of the public. Few appreciations could be farther from the truth than identifying comedy with humor; in fact, they are two visions and two activities very different in life. Comedy is a representation and remains superficial–a spectacle that is perceived immediately and without the need for thought, which quickly passes to our senses. Humor, on the other hand, requires at least a moment of reflection and takes place within us. It is the discovery of the reality we have in front of our eyes, and has a bit of the tragic feeling of existence that makes us smile; the truth that appears unexpectedly with a skeptic face and understanding smile. The guffaw belongs more to comedy; in humor laughter is more subtle, perhaps due to a melancholic disillusion. Humor is an intellectual exercise that has a Western origin and has found its most fertile ground of experimentation in Great Britain. A Christianized country capable of producing the Magna Carta had to have an enormous sense of humor. The most effective instrument in humor appears to be language, and the English have developed a language that is not only a recipient of all lexicons, but is open to the subtle exchange of ideas, perhaps like no other. The connotation the English give to a word during the transmission of thoughts on previously established norms has facilitated the utilization of humor in England and has made the children of Albion the masters of irony. It has also been an effective instrument to recognize each other without the need for introductions: In Great Britain, accent and the method of composing phrases reveals, probably more than anything else, the lineage of an individual. Supreme irreverence challenges the social authority of the monarchy. This type of discourse serves to establish social categories in England with much greater precision than the aristocratic decrees of the crown.

Their language, their peculiar codes of conduct, and the colonization of a large part of this planet, have allowed the English to transmit their style to these colonies. Puritans and agnostics at the same time, the inhabitants of this great European island have demonstrated an extraordinary ability to observe life with irony, and–for several centuries–diplomacy, politics, and social relations on the entire planet have been exposed to the virus of British humor. No one will admit to lacking a sense of humor, and it is rare for a person to confess that their country lacks the appropriate disposition. But contrary to popular belief, humor is accessible to few while comedy is within the reach of the entire world. In spite of the internationality of the term, humor at its best is English, and has produced prototypes that can only be found in London and its vicinities. The rakish and dissipated dandy that lives in an atmosphere of apparent indifference is found in other areas of art and culture–literature, music, politics, etc. However, outside of English-speaking countries, there is no version in the popular landscape that comes close. Across the channel, the "boulevardier blasé," if he exists, in the style of Honore Lachaille or Gaston, could be an imaginary epigenetic but at the most minimal contact with humor, this artificial personality would disappear. In theater, the comedian and the humorist occasionally occupy the same space. Even though it should be quite clear, these two separate outlooks on life are frequently confused with each other. Nietzsche maintains that humor cannot exist within a comedian. This suggestive–and for some perhaps debatable–comment could have some sense to it. Even if there is no other evidence of it, Jerry Lewis is living proof of the basis in the assertion by the German philologist. Though cinema has brought the possibility of collaboration between almost all of the spheres in culture, one of the consequences is that the comedian and the humorist might find themselves participating in the same show. A few years after *Mister Roberts*, Billy Wilder directed a nearly perfect movie: *Some Like It Hot*. In spite of being a comedy, it ends with one of the most memorable humoristic scenes ever seen onscreen. Privileged inheritor of English culture, Ford is not a comedian, but an observer of reality beyond farce. A dandy who approaches humor without going for the guffaw. What he obtained in *Mister Roberts* was a work of sentimental and penetrating irony, a film filled with humor that in movie jargon will continue to be described as a comedy.

Even though filming was filled with mishaps, these are not visible in the final cut. The rhythm that flows through the scenes is impeccable, and there is a wonderful balance between each of the characters as interpreted by the actors. In this film the drama takes place within the characters, so their emotions are only occasionally transmitted to us through extensive dialogues. In certain cases the actions of the protagonists are much more eloquent than their words. Even though the film was based on a stage play, there is not a strong Broadway influence. This was to be expected as John Ford always kept absolute control on the arrangement of the scenery as well as the performance of the actors. During the time this movie was made Ford had reached the pinnacle of his career, and famous movie stars fought for the privilege of acting in his productions. But this director preferred the physical appearance of those who looked the part rather than including them in a movie for their acting abilities. He demanded absolute subordination from the talent for the purposes of the story and never allowed the preferences of the actors to override his own criteria in a production. The violent altercation he had with the actor who portrayed Mr. Roberts might have had something to do with the small authority Ford finally conceded to the stars in the cast. It appears that this incident was the reason the filming was completed by Mervyn LeRoy. In spite of all these difficulties, the actors in *Mister Roberts* accomplish their duties with exemplary efficiency, and each of them gives extraordinary realism to their portrayal. The histrionic versatility displayed by the main actor in *As Good As It Gets*, almost ruining the movie directed by James L. Brooks, would have been inconceivable to attempt with Ford. Unlike the stars in the sky whose reality comes to us through their immense majesty, the brilliance without constancy projected by movie stars never impressed John Ford. In *Mister Roberts* the images of the actors virtually disappear, and all that remains in our imagination are the characters. The actions of the protagonists only reveal their human condition and the temperament of each of the characters gives substance to the story. Morton, the ship's captain, irascible and overbearing, clashes with the

easygoing and pleasant disposition of lieutenant Douglas Roberts, and his popularity guarantees the intervention of other members of the crew in his favor. Frank Pulver, the most timid and respectful of the occupants on the ship, feels compelled to take an inconvenient and symbolic part in the dispute and in the end takes actions unexpected of his character. The ship's doctor, understanding and experienced, acts as a moderating advisor when needed. A sentimental movie nuanced by melancholic humor that leaves an indelible memory in the mind of the viewer and in many of us, the permanent desire to see it again.

The Searchers – 1956

Ten years pass while Ethan Edwards, accompanied
by Martin Pawley, search for his niece, who was
kidnapped by the Comanche when she was a child.
When they locate Debbie they find she is now an
Indian woman living with the man who scalped her
sister and parents. Pawley kills Chief Scar and
Ethan understands and forgives Debbie.

The most eloquent example of John Ford's ideology is a film from his later period. In
The Searchers he traces an intimate journey so that we may come closer to him. This
is also a masterly film, a testament by a man who wants to leave the strength of his
convictions in evidence. A catalogue of everything that he detests and an entire
inventory of his inclinations can be found in this movie. Through it he makes a
precise distinction between what he most respects and the indignity that deserves his
contempt. He has decided to confide in us the essence of his ethics and, just like an
unfaltering Zarathustra, Uncle Ethan will be his terse and stubborn messenger.
Beyond our approval, he seeks our understanding of this courageous and sentimental
centaur. This horseman, who travels the countryside in search of vengeance also
carries the idealism of the director. He doesn't bother to hide his weaknesses, he
contents himself with making certain it is understood that he is a man as straight as a
die. This tenacious and virile figure that gallops to meet his enemies is the incarnation
of John Ford–albeit with two eyes–facing the destiny that approaches. Only time and a
different set of circumstances separate them. The same authority that Ethan exerts on
those who follow him and the admiration he inspires in his family are echoed in the
enthusiasm that Pappy instills on the movie set, and the loyalty and reverence with
which his comrades and collaborators pay homage to him. One of them, a veteran
actor, after decades of playing himself transforms his style so that with moving
devotion he can faithfully project the image of his mentor and friend.

John Ford has made Ethan Edwards into a character as real as himself, a being
without duplicity in his virtues and defects, who is only capable of behaving
according to the principles that he is able to understand, sometimes responding to

spontaneous impulses that later on he will try to rationalize. He might not be very certain about the line separating good and bad, but he knows what his duty is, and no one is going to prevent him from carrying it out. Initially, Ethan rejects Martin Pawley because of his Indian blood, and he doesn't waste any time in getting into a quarrel with Reverend Clayton–as Ethan's spirit does not mix well with the dictates and hypocrisy of religion. His crusade is not associated with any community cause, and responds directly to the conditions and the commitments he has imposed on himself. He doesn't even bother to consider who might be right or wrong. In spite of the rage that the Comanche attack has provoked inside him, he understands that the Indians have lived through many disappointments and have put up with so many offenses. He recognizes the value of these people, but the interests and greed of the wretched sometimes leads to confrontation between the noblest beings. Uncle Ethan is scrupulously loyal and supportive of his own, but he can also be considerate of his adversaries. He would like to be able to separate them from those who are blameless. Nonetheless, war is a miserable game and the vast horizon of the American West is the impassive witness to the massacre.

Ethan Edwards is a man of the land, an energetic and sensible being who has seen history pass before his eyes and has been wounded where it most hurts. He doesn't think he can live without revenge; as it is his only hope to find peace. Neither is he inspired by the charm of a lady, in the usual display of bravery and nobility. The woman capable of calming the fury of his resolution doesn't make an appearance in this film. Following the trail of the pillagers, he travels the entire territory accepting no other law than his freedom of action. This identifies him with his enemy, with whom under other circumstances he would have gotten along well. He goes in search for his niece, a girl who no longer exists as she has grown into a woman. Unable to regain the time lost, there is a desperation in the hate of someone he does not yet know. His grudge is painful, because sometimes it extends to an entire tribe, and deep down he feels a profound respect for the Indians. In any event, he has a self-imposed duty to carry out, and he will do that with an implacable ferociousness. During the development of the plot, racism and rape are shown as the inevitable and natural result of the conflict between the two cultures. Nonetheless, Ethan's determination is born from a higher sentiment: The love for his family. This contradiction betrays the inflexible purpose of his adventure and in the end forces him to be tolerant and understanding.

As the underlying principle of the tragedy, Ford presents us with a confrontation between two worthy positions and the inevitability that one of these must yield without remedy. He takes advantage of the occasion to make evident his contempt for those who propagate the antagonism and benefit from it, without taking sides with either of the parties in conflict. Ethan is also Ford's instrument against man's inhumanity; only the animosity Ethan feels for the Comanche is foreign to the director. Perhaps what Ethan detests most is that the Indians, with whom he has something in common, are the people against whom he must swear vengeance. He understands that the Comanche reaction has grown into hatred of those who have violently snatched something away and knows the conflict is the result of a situation that the Indians were the last to cause. For their part, they feel that it is useless to seek justice when the law has been broken so many times. The irreconcilable perspectives are illustrated in two impressive episodes during the film: The first Comanche attack and the assault by the cavalry toward the end are horrifyingly wretched. The search and dramatic encounter complete the synopsis of the plot. The battle that determines the future of a nation and the disappearance of another is reduced to a microcosm in the confrontation between two individuals of different origins. Neither one can step back nor are they capable of reconciling their respective behavior. The outcome is inevitable, and John Ford establishes himself as arbiter in the quarrel. He doesn't allow Ethan to execute Chief Scar, but gives him a dignified death instead at the hands of Martin Pawley, a member of his own race. During the course of these events, the contrast between the aspirations and perspectives of two different ways of life are revealed with such force that we must reflect on the improbability that the situation could have had any other ending. It is almost as if we are being told that we mustn't blame either side for what is happening.

The conflict between two cultures that do not understand each other is represented by Ford with marvelous simplicity and clarity in *The Searchers*, without taking sides yet trying to understand them in the extreme moments of their tragic confrontation. Ford begins by suggesting that it is trite to refer to moral considerations in a dispute where no one tries to remain within the law, nor is there anyone who trusts it. The life of the Comanche had been subjected to an agreement imposed by force, which had additionally been violated when it suited someone's greed. In their world, where the breach of the orders of the elders would have serious consequences, these homogenous people do not understand the duality of white society, composed of individuals who–either behind the back or with the support of the authorities–act according to their private interests, and whose actions are not controlled by their superiors. The indigenous tribes find it unacceptable to have laws imposed on them by force by a people who later violate these same laws in order to humiliate them. They have not been consulted in establishing these laws of coexistence, nor were they given the opportunity to contribute with their wisdom. They have been forced to accept what was already inconceivable to them: That the earth–that is, nature–is the property of mortal beings, and that these same beings are going to prohibit them from traveling its surface. On the other side, European man, heir to a utilitarian society that tends towards progress, first contemplates his new neighbors with condescension and then is surprised at their resistance in participating in the benefits of progress. Afterwards, he sees an obstacle to the application of the law in the pantheist culture of these people, and feels the forays of these nomad tribes, already beaten down and abused, to be a threat to his security. The conflicting feelings of these cultures remain latent during every moment of the confrontation between the Indian chief and his implacable pursuer. Without offering a chronological explanation to the conflict, nor justifying the events due to the time in which they occur, Ford once again allows all the weight of history to reach our senses.

Unlike music or painting, where ethics do not play a role, morals become an important protagonist in literature and movies. With the help of these two expressions of culture and from experience we have learned that liberty, dignity and honor are three terms that have little significance for those with pontifical certainty: Those who think they know what is right or wrong, what benefits each person, and are confident of being able to give the entire world what it deserves. Far from doing that, in each of his films Ford pays tribute to those virtues that have made Western civilization possible, providing the grounds for romanticism. In his films, the images that stand out with admirable clarity symbolize two currents of thinking and ethics that have for centuries been learning to coexist, and differ as much in their origin as in their destiny: The messianic socialist of biblical origin and pagan European liberalism. More than two thousand years ago, in the fluid Mediterranean frontier, their meeting took place. One of them is ascribed to the temple parishioners, who came from the desert and venerate the prophet. Through their faith they have found virtue in their beliefs and finality in their ceremonies. In permanent direct communication with God, they are gregarious and without the need to conspire they react to the common impulse in unison like bees from the same hive. The others are creatures of the forest, disciples that go as far as the agora in search of knowledge and who respect the teacher; they doubt and formulate questions freely, giving significance to their ideals. They are the descendents of myth; they love the land upon which they stand. The others are the offspring of dogma and believe that the entire planet belongs to them. Ford outlines the conflict through simple and accessible characters. He leans toward the individualistic and anonymous hero, while demonstrating as well a thoughtful respect toward the institutions that give refuge to the indigent human being. Inside the world of John Ford, the dignity of the free and honest man prevails, regardless of his defects or the accumulation of his errors. In the end, only opportunism and hypocrisy remain as villains.

In contrast to the sympathy Ford shows Scar, as arrogant and warlike as he is, is the aversion he feels for Futterman, the trader. The maliciousness, deception, and hypocrisy that are so concentrated in this individual are the antithesis to the principles that John Ford supports. An ominous figure, he belongs to another social order and looks down with superiority upon those that view him with contempt; he lies in wait in the shadows for their fall and aspires to be the ferocious worm within their lifeless and defeated corpses. Ford first introduces him in the film as an intrusion, in order to have the pleasure of exterminating this vermin. And he does so with relish in the most offensive manner he can find for those of this species: Demonstrating Futterman's lack of cunning and inferiority. The scenes of the encounter between Ethan and Pawley and the trader are a form of execution of the latter, a delicate demonstration of cynicism towards hypocrisy and they are totally unnecessary. They do not contribute to the narration in any way, nor do they have any effect on the dynamic of the story. *The Searchers* is a long saga with a brief intermission in the narration that could be titled *Presenting Mr. Futterman*. The decision to include the scenes with this individual is quite revealing in an intimate and unusual way, as Ford had never before been the one to personally execute a character he created. In his films, death is an eventuality that ensues as a consequence of the circumstances, and it is these that determine the end of each life. Ford always allows events to occur according to the demands of logic, avoiding everything that does not give coherence to the narrative. The Futterman episode can only be interpreted as a strategy he used to tell us about himself, a tool to demonstrate his disapproval of a phony and crooked individual, and his scorn for everything he represents. In *Cheyenne Autumn* Ford makes a similar digression, but it is with the purpose of emphasizing the dissipation of the nascent towns of the Wild West in contrast to the poverty of the Indians a couple of miles in the distance, and the indifference of the white people to their suffering. This time, John Ford makes a parenthesis in *The Searchers* to mock the image of a detestable being and to let us in on his opinion of his methods, staging a sordid scene that has very little to do with the clear skies and open spaces of the plains of the Comanche.

In the conflicts he represents, Ford endeavors to penetrate the minds of the participants to better understand their reactions. He adjusts his judgment to their instincts and identifies with the passions that give life to the protagonists. The inclinations of each of the characters as seen through their actions are consistent with their personalities. The viewer always feels certain of the way each of the different characters portrayed by John Ford is going to behave. Before deciding to film this passionate odyssey, the director of *Fort Apache* and *Rio Grande* would refuse to introduce into his movies individuals who did not properly respond to an anticipated pattern of conduct. However, with *The Searchers* he explores psychological paths that had not previously been a focal point of his camera and approaches individuals who have a human condition unlike anything that had interested him to this point. Prior to *The Searchers*, insanity, homosexuality, sadism, and other undesirable abnormalities of nature that have been the components or themes in movies by other directors did not inhabit John Ford's world. There is no doubt that in this movie his intention is to alter the norms he had followed throughout his stories and introduce symbols that did not properly belong at the core of the narration but that serve on this occasion to dramatize the setting. In the film, aside from Futterman's congenital perversity, there is the sporadic appearance of Mose Harper, a secondary personality clearly affected by dementia. With the presence of this individual, the director attempts to illustrate the dreadful trauma suffered by some as a result of the savagery of the conflict. It is not that there were fundamental changes to the structure of *The Searchers* compared to other movies by this director, but it is true that this intimate and revealing film did not faithfully follow the traditional treatment Ford's cinema had given westerns previously.

The anomalous characters introduced in this movie serve to emphasize the vision of the hero who must fulfill the ideals of the director. But not even for an instant can it be considered that Ford realized an autobiographical work in *The Searchers*. There is no tendency further from the temperament of this insightful observer of the complex human condition than exhibitionism. However, he has no reservations in showing us something more internal about himself and, in an act of supreme generosity, he wants to share with us his doubts and convictions. Even though his purpose isn't to bring attention to himself, with the help of Ethan Edwards, he does wish to confide his thoughts. Along with these reflections, there is a self-analysis of the principles that he has upheld throughout his life. He refuses to keep the mysteries of his mind secret and reveals them to us with veiled modesty through one of the most clearly defined characters in film. By situating Edwards inside an epic context, there is no restraint in the representation of the image. Ford develops the drama and places his alter ego in the middle of a historically transcendental conflict. He does so in order to show that, at any moment, a man's actions and thoughts can make him the center of the universe. Passion and sacrifice are shown with the greatest intensity in this saga inspired by the wish for revenge. An impartial conductor of the drama, Ford directs the actions of the participants and makes them behave according to their nature. Some consider this movie to be the pinnacle work of his career. *The Searchers* is surely one of the most intimate and personal of his films. The epilogue takes place off-screen and in our minds. It is like an allegory of ethical behavior for each of us: Even if perfection isn't within our reach, we are obligated to pursue it.

The Last Hurrah – 1958

Frank Skeffington's final mayoral campaign in a town
in New England. The mayor confronts the aristocracy
of the community who this time defeats him.

John Ford's heroes appear to be above adversity. Defeat barely diminishes their
optimism, and humor protects them from becoming discouraged. It's as if each of
them had a reserve of energy born from the deepest of their convictions. Almost all
of them have something of Ford's idealist spirit. But few represent him as faithfully
as this mayor, who is also Irish, and like Ford, born in New England. If Uncle Ethan
in *The Searchers* was the image of the director in the middle of a savage conflict
between two cultures, Skeffington in *The Last Hurrah* is his alter ego within the
sophisticated manipulations of politics. Frank is a firm believer in the vital force of
tradition, and his customary electoral victories are its results. He is convinced that
the town will have to pay a high price when it decides to change that which has been
constructed over time. According to his criteria he should remain as mayor, because
his presence forms a part of the tradition and his continuity guarantees the
community's success. Experienced and realistic, he realizes his electoral possibilities
are diminishing. While his followers get ready to celebrate another victory, he
decides to prepare for his first defeat. He is the only one who is conscious of the
impending disaster and, a pragmatist to the end, wants to extract any advantage from
what will be his last, frustrated attempt. In the electoral fiasco he sees an
educational opportunity for his nephew and invites him to witness his defeat against
an inept opponent. He names the incompetent son of his adversary honorary fire
chief and in doing so obtains considerable funds for the urban projects Skeffington
had been trying to secure for some of the more disadvantaged zones of the city.

This story takes place when there was still some imagination in the decisions made by
those in government, prior to the monstrous growth that made bureaucracies the
dictators of politics. At the time, the ends justified the means and we could still trust the
honesty and good faith of the politicians. Back then voters in America preferred to stick
by the human condition of the aspirant rather than the efficiency of ideologies. Now
elected candidates arrive to power depending upon life-long employees of the state that

manage the bureaucratic machinery, which is why today countries are not governed by statesmen, but by ignorant bureaucrats with an enormous amount of accumulated information. There was a sense of camaraderie behind the maneuvers candidates, then and now, have felt inclined to practice. First technology and then population growth have contributed to its disappearance from the political panorama. At the same time that Skeffington's last campaign was taking place, television was becoming a formidable instrument of propaganda. As a consequence, there was a change in the process and in the electoral tactics. Romantic and perseverant once again, Ford fixes his camera on the end of an era that was extinguished during his lifetime and manages to create a character that is difficult to believe belongs to fiction. It feels as if his actions are taking place at the same time we are observing the movie. In addition to being an amazing movie, *The Last Hurrah* is a sentimental homage to a political style that is gone forever.

Frank Skeffington is a local figure, but possesses the aptitudes and intuitive talents of a true politician. He looks to the outside while at the same time he strives to transform his surroundings. He isn't at all like the abject bureaucrat who only considers his own personal necessities and accepts whatever is needed to satisfy them. Bureaucracy and politics are two activities that almost always begin on the same path, but whose ultimate purposes differ fundamentally. Without considering the distance that separates them in their irreconcilable aspirations, the first is inactive and the second tends to be dynamic. Those who act purely on bureaucratic ambitions do not have a true political vocation. It is important to specify the difference between these two notions in order to distinguish the intentions of our representatives: A politician's actions must have the purpose of changing the living conditions of the sector he represents and to improve their future, while the opportunism of the bureaucrat advises keeping everything static so that, from his privileged position, he can take credit for what he has tried to prevent and others have achieved. This specimen is like a bird of little imagination and short flight that only appears during moments of success and takes advantage of the town's inability to recognize his wretched behavior. It is important to classify and give a specific denomination to the activities of politicians and bureaucrats within government. Otherwise, terms start to get mixed up, and causes and effects end up confused: Chickens think the sun comes up because the rooster crows. That is the source of the prestige of this arrogant fowl in the corral.

The route of a politician from anonymity to popularity is filled with temptations that will test his true vocation. During the journey to the position that will allow him to exercise some authority, the politician lives through periods that are like two faces of the same coin. One of them is useful in attracting a larger amount of followers and reaches the desired position. Once he feels he has sufficient faculties to put his projects in motion, the other face will come to light. If within his plans he contemplates risking his well-being to give life to his ideals, the public official will reveal his political intentions. If on the other hand he prefers to conform and use the position he occupies to protect his personal gains and remain there indefinitely, then he will probably become a high-ranking bureaucrat. The journey to positions of public responsibility and the exercise of authority are also plagued by dangers that can transform a popular leader into a political failure. It is unfortunate that the average citizen will only learn the intentions of the contender after he has taken office. By then, it is usually too late. That is why, prior to backing the candidate, rather than considering their party affiliation or listening to their promises, it is essential to analyze personal inclinations with considerable care and demand integrity from the individual who aspires to represent us.

There is no doubt that politics has had considerable effect on history, but at the same time history has had a powerful effect on politics. Just as our time determines the living conditions to be inherited by future generations, how we live today is also a consequence of the social structures created in the past. The latter half of the nineteenth century was assaulted by a series of theories that promised solutions for the future of humanity. These almost supernatural utopias spread across the planet during the first part of the following century, while the reality of industrialization became tangible. The impact of the First World War cast out these fascinating solutions and only Marxism and psychoanalysis survived–and with a pseudo intellectual varnish they became products for mass consumption. The radiant communist promise has been defeated, and every day there is growing skepticism on the merits of the other. That abundance of liberating ideas which should have filled us with hope did not provide the results expected by the revolutionary optimists. The demagoguery of those who took advantage of the opportunity offered by the Treaty of Versailles and the hysteria of others prevented the open debate that might have freed humanity from the horrors of the Second World War. This war began with optimistic omens that announced wonderful solutions for future societies and promised an end to all tyrannies. But after the most devastating and bloody conflict in history, the opportunism of certain groups finished off any remaining possibilities of discussing ideas or making culture available to all and preparing society for future scientific advances. By choosing the use of armament sixty-five years ago, politics abandoned culture in favor of an ocean of information and entirely bureaucratized itself. As a result, what could have been the dawn of modern thought and a new beginning of rationalism became a setting for comedians and well-informed chatterboxes. The effects of the horrific holocaust paralyzed intelligent evolution in modern society. Today, nothing impels the governing sector to seek the advice of the intellectual observer, nor does a politician feel the need to discern between the trivial and that which is destined to fulfill an essential role in the future of humanity. There is no desire to even listen to the disturbing echoes of the voices of Joseph Campbell, Leni Riefenstahl, Gore Vidal, and Umberto Eco. We have paid a dear price for not being able to destroy that ominous totalitarianism without resorting to war, as we did later on with the Soviet threat. The consequences have been the interruption of philosophical dialogue, which gave demagoguery more room to work and, eventually, under the auspices of an unobjectionable presidential and parliamentary system, the masses have achieved maximum–predominance. This is at the expense of the individual who has lost a portion of his freedom. Even though that might not have been his intention, the most accurate conclusion on humanity's disposition towards the problems it faces was made by Jimmy Durante in two words a few decades ago when he asked, "What elephant?"

In *The Last Hurrah* the debate takes place at a municipal level where political decisions have a more direct impact on the citizenry and the activities of the candidate are less conditioned to the interests of a specific group. The movie reflects the political life of one of these irreverent and straightforward exchanges that allows us to more easily distinguish the demagogue from the true politician. Diplomats who move with ease on the international stage or those who develop their political activity in the lap of national government obtain greater popularity, but that does not mean that the governing body of a small city, by representing a smaller amount of people, has a lesser degree of responsibility. Mahatma Gandhi and his project for India, General George Marshall and his plan for the countries devastated by war, or a mayor who offers solutions to his municipality willingly acquire identical moral commitment. The ethical condition of a leader is not determined by the expanse of the field in which he operates but by the solidity of his convictions and the sacrifice he is willing to proffer to defend them. Political activity has been described in many different ways: War through nonviolence; action within what is possible in defense of an ideal, etc. These definitions only partially address the subject, but might be of help in clearing up certain confusions. The first notion disqualifies the administrator who feels the need to resort to war to attain the results that can be obtained through a negotiable disposition. Even if he is victorious in the conflict, he will be a failed politician the moment battle begins. The second classification describes the politician analyzed in retrospect, whose actions have already passed into history. In any event, political activity on its various levels will always be undergoing a definition process and remain a subject for discussion.

During the first part of the past century, Europe was engulfed in a political discussion posed by socialism, while the United States distinguished itself for being the country least susceptible to the influence of this new doctrine. By remaining indifferent to the socialist proposals championed by the disciples of Marx, a different political scene was developing in America. A country accustomed to the spectacular results obtained by individual action was not very receptive to a collective solution that offered a "proletariat social revolution," where "man's exploitation of man" was going to be carried out in reverse and the "comrade" epithet would substitute all other forms of address. In addition to having whatever significance anyone wanted to give "comrade"… to obtain these lofty purposes would require the extermination of half of the population on the planet! Christianity and socialism share the same messianic source. From the first edition of *Capital* some European thinkers anticipated the confrontation between the Evangel and the Communist Manifesto would be either fortuitous or artificial, but the American public was the first to suspect that Providence and Communism come from the same idea put into a different context. Appealing to the masses seems a bit absurd in a continent that offered so many opportunities to the individual. The solemn Marxist formula would not incite much enthusiasm in this informal and prosperous setting. America had already found a style and adopted a code of conduct within its constitution, and this was an argument worth defending within the political debate. The great contribution of the United States was to give the electoral process an undertone of athletic competition that the rest of the countries have imitated in some measure. The leaders, just like the athletes in this country, were arriving from the universities, which is why the political rivalries here have something of a collegiate competition to them. Because voters pay more attention to the pragmatic positions of the candidates than to their ideologies, their personal qualities and personal behavior acquire greater attention. The physical appearance and the personality of a government hopeful are usually the determining factors when it comes time to count the votes. This peculiarity of the political scene in North America is a fascinating field of exploration for literature, a rich vein for professional biographers and a gold mine for the tabloids. Literary activities like the ones mentioned here also provide cinema with the elements that a historical document hardly ever contains. Those intimate fragments of a personality that give life to historical figures are found by cinema in novels and casual reports generally not chronicled by historians. Perhaps the dates recorded are not very reliable and might have been altered by popular account, but without recurring to people's imagination, history is only an accumulation of data. In *The Last Hurrah*, the usual occurrences in the electoral process are narrated by someone who appears to have observed them from behind the scenes. Possibly during his youth in New England, John Ford might have had the opportunity to closely observe some of those charismatic politicians, so familiar to the townships that elected them.

Two philosophies crossed the ocean almost simultaneously to influence two disproportionate segments of the American continent. From the extreme southwest of Europe to the southern area of the New World comes the Holy Inquisition, with its religious morality of Arab ancestry and Hispanic inflection. Its foundation is solidly backed by the set of laws that proclaim the well-known Ten Commandments. Following its emissaries, the most extensive colonization begun at the end of the fifteenth century generated social organizations and governments in which The Inquisition was the determining influence in their structure. While in the northern part of the continent, civil society, also religious but more disassociated from the Church, granted the people the right to participate within an entirely different governmental system. This British aspiration, born in the spirit of Greece with the wisdom of Roman law and summarized in the Magna Carta, has as its main purpose the protection of free thought and the preservation of the government that will allow its expression. According to its stipulations, beyond freedom of expression we will only encounter tyranny and darkness. The libertarian Anglo-Saxon proposal offers everything that the principles that inspired the standards of the governments derived from the Inquisition do not. According to them, outside of religion we are only going to wallow in sin, which leads to licentiousness and anarchy. We see how during the beginning of the colonization of a continent that extends from one pole of the planet to the other bases its social structures on two completely different premises. The absolutist minds, in favor of the use of force to impose doctrine, found the best area for expansion to be the part that extends south from the Rio Bravo to Patagonia. The two countries situated to the north built a less authoritarian society that encouraged a more open political debate and founded a system of government that a twentieth-century politician described as being the worse... except for all others. In this portion of the continent, Frank Skeffington has the opportunity to display his powers of persuasion and talents at governing, and his activities take place when the country's institutions had already proven their efficiency. The methods and personality of the mayor respond perfectly to the typical image of an American politician from the first part of the last century.

Skeffington is a liberal politician, though not a socialist. He wants the community to freely respond to the call to conscience, so that each individual may aspire to better opportunities. He doesn't believe that social position or economical situations affect the moral condition of a person or alter human nature. Neither does he expect spectacular solutions through the application of some theory, nor does he imagine that the opportunism of some might be corrected by the simple act of belonging to a particular political party. His humanism leads him to favor those in need, but he resists placing his conscience at the service of those who swear they have the formula to remedy all of society's problems. The mayor is sufficiently intuitive to not take the Marxist dogma seriously, and too liberal to trust any dictatorship, even a proletarian one. His individualistic approach distances him even further from the egalitarian doctrine that seduced so many at the time. In spite of the link that has taken place within the English language between the terms liberalism and socialism, in reality these are two opposing concepts that the director of this film never allowed to be confused. Two voices of different origin collide in their meaning as well as in the purposes of those who interpret them. The essence of liberalism already appears in classical philosophy. It is present in the Roman Senate, it is energetically evident in debate in the British Parliament, it drives American independence and becomes popular during the French Revolution. If in the slogans of that revolution, the word "freedom" had not been accompanied by two other entelechies–equality and fraternity–that vain Corsican midget would not have been able to use it and eventually pervert it. That particular betrayal was not something that Voltaire or Rousseau would have dreamt of or what would have inspired Beethoven in his Heroic Symphony. Let's continue deliberating; the liberal is for the dignity and the value of the individual and does not accept subordination to the masses. The socialist, on the other hand, is doctrinal and in favor of collectively enforcing reforms. They claim to be on the side of the people, but in reality they only generate bureaucracy and corrupt it even more. Socialism has its roots in religion and in the nineteenth century arises from theories with the purpose of subverting order and replacing one doctrine with another not much different. It frequently falls into fascism and can even find common ground among conservatives, but its ideological approximation to liberal thought is inconceivable. To introduce the term "liberal" where the descriptive "socialist" should be used makes dialogue incomprehensible, debate difficult, and sinks any conversation about politics into chaos. And that is exactly what is happening now.

To classify as liberal, as it is done in the United States, those who declare themselves in favor of conceding greater power or more funds to bureaucracy doesn't make any sense. To confuse liberalism with socialism is an aberration, although socialists are quite happy with the classification to better conceal their intentions. Liberalism was conceived to stimulate free thought in every individual and in opposition to tyranny. It does not promise anything and knows it will have to continue to fight for the freedom of investigation and analysis. Otherwise there is no hope for the future. Its ideals and goals are incorruptible, because the true liberal does not aspire to power, only to limit it. The Latin root of the term is of noble origin and has left an indelible mark in the vocabulary of all languages. It remains associated to the ideas of "independence," "freedom," "liberty," "autonomy," "liberation," "sovereignty," "emancipation," "individuality," and all other derivatives. Appropriately used, the verb "liberal" can never be conjugated as a pejorative, but in an edifying sense. Socialism, on the other hand, has an absolutist and messianic ancestry. It looks to control the individual and convenes multitudes as mobs or, even better, as a flock. The liberal rejects dogma in all of its manifestations; the socialist only opposes it because it wants to impose another. The similarity that some believe there to be between these two opposite ideas has an explanation in history: During one episode the two were united in their opposition to governments allied with the Church and were the object of indiscriminate persecution. This precarious historical synchrony caused religion and authority to identify ancient liberalism with incipient socialism from then on, ignoring the profound differences that existed between these repressed movements. Even so, at no time has there been any obvious coincidence between the purposes and methods that characterize these two clearly opposite tendencies. Although the conservative bourgeoisie has not bothered to differentiate these positions and Marxism hasn't been interested in being set apart and is quite comfortable with the dignified designation of liberal, the goals of socialism and liberalism are diametrically opposed. The confusion of one for the other is only possible not knowing the past of these political movements and ignoring the origin of each of these two terms. Trying to equate them ideologically is an assault against etymology and against history.

There are those who contend that in order to be a true Bostonian you must be of Irish ancestry and to become an authentic American politician, you must be born in Boston. We can assume that Skeffington possessed both conditions and had the characteristics expected of a leader of his time. He also has within him the necessary attributes of a true leader. As it is not possible to satisfy everyone, he is forced, more often than he would like, to compromise his principles but without renouncing his fundamental objective. The mayor, who is preparing to be the protagonist of his "last hurrah," knows that perfection within power is a dream, because relativity will always be a factor, as much in the analysis of the problems as in the political decisions. Differences within the city council are generally reduced to the way to use or distribute constituent funds. Debate is open on a daily basis, but sometimes there are personal attacks and deceptions. It is an environment rich with the mixture of rivalries and camaraderie, and this circumstance provides situations and dialogues saturated with humor that are characteristic of the cinema of John Ford. The director has found a character he understands, with whom he can identify and sketch the image of a true politician, not that of an orator who preaches transcendental pretensions of no substance. We know how Skeffington will behave in any situation and, even though his activities will take place in a peaceful setting, we have no doubt that the mayor will always be on top of the circumstances in the event of an emergency of any kind.

On several occasions Hollywood has made excursions into the unstable world of politics and, in this complicated setting of conflicting interests, the common denominator of those films is usually the episode where the characters find themselves obligated to pronounce themselves duty-bound in the face of a profound crisis of the conscience. In the cinema of other countries, the moral sacrifice that is sometimes required by politics from a leader has also developed as a subject. In a single scene in *The Boxer* the stoic condition that must be maintained by someone who represents others is masterly illustrated when the circumstances place him in the predicament of having to make a decision under extreme conditions: Near the end of the movie, the leader of the armed coalition is forced to sacrifice one of his own in order to avoid greater harm to their cause. This political measure becomes the climax of the story and is also the ending of the movie by John Sheridan. The quarrels of the city council in New England are not life and death. Nonetheless, the true politician must give proof of being so in all latitudes and under every circumstance. From his death bed, Skeffington has the fortune of seeing some of his projects materialize. There is nothing more he can do and he only wishes to find out "how it is possible to be thankful for an eternal smile." The final sequences of the film appear to be a metaphor of our journey through life, which begins with a brief happy welcome followed by a prolonged and sad farewell.

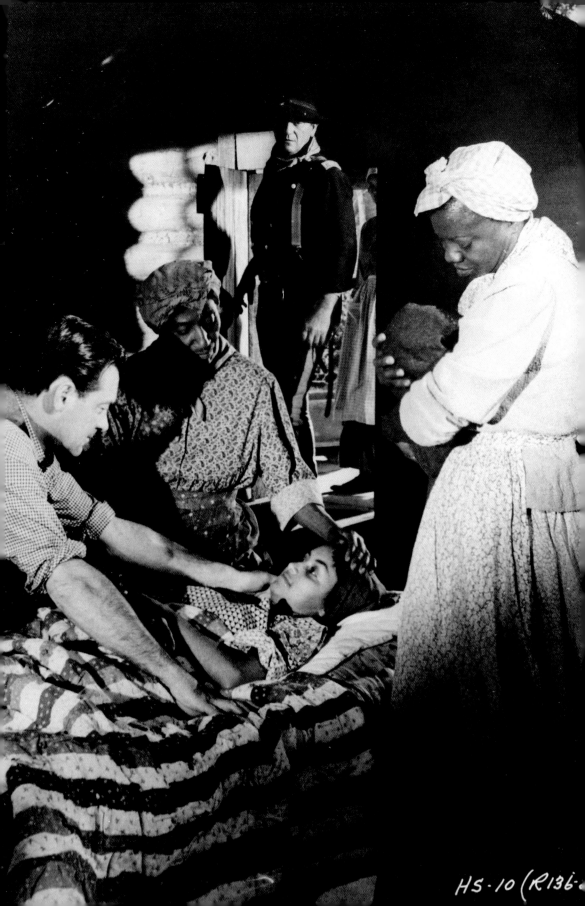

The Horse Soldiers – 1959

Colonel John Marlowe begins a military campaign
behind the lines of the Confederate army. Hannah
Hunter, his lover and a supporter of the South,
overhears his battle plans. To avoid the plans from
being passed to the enemy, the colonel must keep
her and her slave with him. Mayor Doctor
Kendall, with whom the colonel has had some
differences, takes care of him when he is injured,
and Marlowe promises to return with Hannah
when the war is over.

The American Civil War is the departure point from which almost all of John
Ford's cinematography takes place. It is after that conflict when history begins
to further feed the imagination of the most prolific director cinema has ever
had, and almost all of his stories take place either at the end of the bloody
struggle or during the years in which he lived. *The Horse Soldiers* deals with
one of the last skirmishes during that war. The film exposes in a schematic way
the reasons for the battle, the principles that each of the factions believes to be
defending, and offers us the opportunity to examine them from opposing
perspectives. Within the poignant panorama presented, the conviction that drove
each side and the determination with which they defended ideals contrary to
those of their adversaries is highlighted. The subject could have been shown
with spectacular cinematographic display in the style of the great productions
of that time. But it is a rare moment when lavish leads to excellence, and the
director did not intend to sacrifice the quality of the film in benefit of the
public's preferences. The lack of willingness by John Ford to make concessions
in order to satisfy the taste of the masses must have been infuriating to
producers. The filming took place with great commercial expectations, which is
why he obtained the participation of two of the most in demand actors of that
time for *The Horse Soldiers*. It is understood that movie stars are a lure for the
attending public who view the images of their idols, and the advertisement of
their names is what fills theaters. To compete in the box office, an extravagant

film was expected, but John Ford favored a making a less ostentatious but more intimate and moving film. Its ethical content places this movie in the company of *Cheyenne Autumn* and *The Searchers*, and for the moving realism of its scenes it deserves to be classified among the best in Ford's cinema. If it had been presented as an impressive military production rather than a touching human reflection on the consequences of war, perhaps the public's response might have been more enthusiastic and the movie might have garnered a much greater but temporary success. In any event, to see *The Horse Soldiers* is an experience that produces an unforgettable impact in the viewer. These horsemen who traveled through the South prior to their westward march would soon leave a deep imprint upon the country–episodes that cinematography would continue to recall during the next century.

The film is a rebuke of those who prefer to observe history casually in order to accommodate their opinion to the more convenient position of the moment, but there is a realistic alternative that allows a more neutral analysis of that struggle. This is found in John Ford's film. Ruined plantations observe the passage of the horsemen, whom, from then on, the defeated will be forced to obey. Those desolate and opulent mansions are the residue of the incomparable prosperity from that period. Some of the scenes are heart-rending. Children, the last reserve of a proud populace, beg for the privilege of marching to the front lines. The outcome of the conflict freed the slaves and would restore dignity to half of the country, but had an exorbitant cost for everyone. The white settlers of the American South no longer had to carry the embarrassing stigma that proclaiming themselves the owners of the bodies and lives of other living beings signifies, but would have to pay for the result of the war with their impoverishment. The bloody confrontation that mutilated an economy based on slavery put an end to the economic boom in the entire American South and had other sad consequences as well: Those with darker skin where not yet prepared to develop freely and lost the only sustenance and shelter their humiliating dependence had provided. The more audacious marched towards the large metropolises in search of a more promising future, while others decide to remain close to the land where they were born, without future and condemned to misery. In its dynamic brutality, war destroys lives and devastates sectors of production. It doesn't make any distinctions in what it comes across. Avoiding war is the most essential requirement of a politician who aspires to deserve this description. The true statesman must know that to preserve peace, a leader shouldn't be too insistent or excessively ambitious in his objectives. One must accept that governments are incapable of forcing constituents to be fair with one another. The best that authority can do is protect everyone's rights. Perhaps the document that speculates on this subject has never been authored, but it would be fascinating to know if a brilliant statesman might have been able to manage the emancipation of people of color without having to pay the painful cost of a battle between fellow countrymen.

There are so many undiscovered aspects of human nature. As in analyzing history, the interest in searching for the truth within in it is subjected to the sensibility and honesty of each chronicler. The capacity to penetrate the minds of those depicted depends on the intuition of the investigator. As David Hume has noted, the authentic historian has to find the truth behind the lies created by interests and passions while logically and honestly interpreting the events. Rather than entertaining the public with spectacular military display, Ford endeavors to fill the void left by historians and concentrate his attention on the personalities of the characters. He might not have been rigorously faithful to the historical text, but through his camera everything seems to make more sense. History is almost always written with the preoccupation that the judgments of the victorious prevail. Without perseverant critics to keep watch, history would end up being a lie. The artist that entertains his imagination with these details forms part of the dissidence necessary for impartial analysis of the historic document. Even though anecdotes are generally of little interest to a historian, the movie director has always made use of them. The internal world of the military has generally passed unnoticed to those who are only interested in the final result of the conflict. Here, as in another of his movies, Ford immerses us into a disciplined military organization, to allow us to observe any discrepancy that might exist in its core. In this film those differences acquire a sentimental connotation as the narrative unfolds.

As always, then and now, defeat emerges from the war showing its horrified and pained countenance, while the victors hurry to cover it up with the seductive mask of victory. The bloody outcome of the last battle disrupted the morale of command of the troops that arrived to suppress the stronghold of the enemy, and victory is overshadowed by the heartbreaking spectacle at the end of the conflict. The bloody defeat suffered by the Confederate Army makes the officials on the winning side reflect on the justification of this or any other war. The result of the combat has shaken the conscience of each of the participants. Their opposing functions within the same army motivate Doctor Kendall and Colonel Marlowe to contemplate these events from different perspectives. One strives to observe the panorama from a strictly military position while Mayor Kendall's medical profession prevails on his judgment and inclines him toward a less political and more humanitarian disposition. Both men face the same circumstances but are incapable of reconciling their respective ways of thinking. Their disagreement is exacerbated by other personal factors, and even though their relationship is not harmonious, they must respond to the situation with the respect and loyalty required by the military.

Without delving into the reasons for the struggle, the director probes the emotional intimacy of the protagonists. Given the extreme situation of the bloody conflict, personal feelings give way to the allegiance that each must devote to their cause, and in this context the political differences that separate Colonel Marlowe and his lover, Hannah Hunter, is the metaphor of a war that never should have happened. It is possible that the sentimental relationship between them and their opposing political positions were factors that captured John Ford's interest in this story. Ford was an American of deep convictions and a professional committed to his work. He didn't let his own political tendencies prevail upon his duty to his country, nor did he let his personal preferences affect the results of his work. As was his habit, he maintained an impartial position during the story, without making assertions on the quarrel that bloodied the two sides of our country during the latter half of the nineteenth century. The director shows respect for the defeated, who–right or wrong–were capable of sacrificing themselves for a cause. He also pays equal tribute to the victorious. The objectives of John Ford's analysis are the consequences of that devastating confrontation and the effects it had on the minds of the protagonists. Two male movie stars portray the dynamic portion of the film; even so, it is the almost-secondary actors and actresses who depict some of the more touching parts of the narrative. The convictions of the prominent Colonel John Marlowe appear as almost irrelevant abstractions when compared to the anguished pleas of the child–nearly anonymous–who wishes to participate in the sacrifice of his people. This childlike determination to march towards death is what gives an even more accurate impression of the foolishness of war. In another scene, confronted with the affectionate consideration shown by Hannah Hunter for Lukey, Doctor Kendall, and Colonel Marlowe cannot help feeling ashamed of their disputes. The plantation lady and her slave do not allow the social change that is being heralded to alter the nature of their friendship, and the new rules will do nothing but strengthen the caring affection that unites them. Recent regulations and the abolition of slavery are insignificant details in comparison to the deep reciprocal respect that exists between them. Women maintain closer contact with the earth that ensures the future of humanity. Their

maternal vocation provides a more realistic vision of life and predisposes them to better handle themselves during times of crisis. Compared to the transcendental purpose of maternity, the violent disagreements between men seem like senseless, dangerous, and childish games. This half of our species considers it absurd that laws should dictate the course of an individual's feelings. Hannah and Lukey do not let the circumstances affect the nature of their personal relationship, and even when the new regulations would tend to separate them, the affection they feel for each other will keep them together until death.

It isn't fair to appraise a work of art only taking into consideration its commercial results. In film, as in any other artistic presentation, one mustn't ignore the viewer's tendency to value the incidental over the substance of what the artist has obtained. Confusing the superficial aspects of an object with its true significance is a very common predisposition among many who attend various types of art events. This is why there usually exists an abysm of incomprehension between the intention of the person who creates a painting or a sculpture and the point of view of the observer. Taste is generally somewhat subjective, which is to say that it depends on the individual and their preferences. On the other hand, quality in art is invariable and is not conditioned to the disposition of the spectator, but is inherent to the content and essence of the work. A symphony by Beethoven could seem to some an unbearable noise, but when it penetrates a certain sensibility in others it acquires a magical significance, and sometimes it has an effect that transcends beauty and rises to the sublime. In Rembrandt's painting there is an intrinsic value in the execution that is aside from the taste of the viewer. The merit of his painting does not depend on the subject he portrays, be it the magnificent head of a noble Fleming or the carcass of a cow. It is not the object that is essential, but the feeling the artist put into it during its realization. This elemental way of observing art appears to be something that escapes the comprehension of many people. Exploration through technique and image to find something of true creative power depends on a certain degree of sensibility, and this desire to identify with the purpose of the artist is a condition that is not present in most. The author of something must follow the course of his own inspiration. If there is an interest in his ideas, it will be the spectator who will try to connect with the innovative thought, because an artist cannot make concessions without degrading his work. In addition to a favorable disposition by a viewer, the "journey to the land of the poet"* requires comprehension of any creative effort; understanding its significance has obstacles of diverse natures. To be able to properly value a work of art requires time, something not everyone has available. Aside from this limitation, the messages the public receives on this subject aren't always worthy of consideration and, on occasion, can even be contradictory. In film, technology has so much influence on the final result and specialization has reached such extremes that it is even more difficult to determine the value of a movie. Nowadays we can view movies that are nearly perfect, even though they are insufferable from their opening

*From Goethe: "Wer den Dichter will verstehen, Muss in Dichters Lande gehen"

scenes. Sort of like those plastic apples that are superior in appearance to real fruit, but that nobody would ever eat. The cinema of John Ford is the opposite of the ornamental artifice so common within a performance that only looks to impress by the shine on its surface. In *The Horse Soldiers*, we can't help being touched by a powerful human depth that beats under the slight and almost trivial representation of history.

Sergeant Rutledge – 1960

> During a court martial, a black sergeant accused of murder is defended by the young lieutenant Tom Cantrell. He proves Rutledge's innocence and in the process discovers the real perpetrator of the rape and murder.

John Ford showed his affection in a very personal way that some perhaps were justified in considering as extravagant. He enjoyed inconveniencing movie stars (even if some of them were his friends) while at the same time exhibiting great gentleness with the less-prominent actors and actresses who formed part of the cast. In his personal circle, he apparently preferred the company of Irishmen, those who appeared to be, or–according to his peculiar criteria–acted as such. Whatever his reasons for his personal preferences, through his habits and his work one can feel the important significance friendship held for him. During his frequent scouting for exterior locations, he met several descendants of indigenous tribes and established some strong friendships. It is said that some of the movies filmed on Indian reservations were done so with the needs of these people in mind. It is conceivable that the fascination he held for Monument Valley, the friendly relationships he had with the inhabitants there, and the friendship that bound him to the actor who would portray Rutledge, encouraged him to film this story. Ford's elevated concept of loyalty could have had something to do with his decision to film a movie in the vicinity of that landscape inhabited by his native friends. The story mostly takes place in a setting suitable to the dynamism of the typical western. But in its conception, execution, and outcome the movie is really a tribute to human solidarity. The central theme develops within the core of a small community in the American West protected by the cavalry. A crime is committed by one of its citizens, and civic interests, prejudices, and a hurried investigation incorrectly places the blame upon the sergeant. It is possible that this soldier was once a slave displaced by the turbulence of the Civil War and who after his emancipation manages to find freedom and shelter within the Army. Inside the military discipline and the risks of everyday life he finds a place for his battered dignity, and in the wide plains creates a future of emancipation and well-being previously denied to him. The accusations of rape and homicide made against him bring his illusions crashing down to earth and transform him into a disappointed being without hope. The brave sergeant feels he no longer has anyone to offer his loyalty and sacrifice. Circumstances and the determination of a young, valiant, and romantic official help him in the end to reconcile with the world of the white man where he thought he belonged at one point. The American West always seems to offer hope and courage to those who risk themselves under its skies. Deception has a short life for those who stride through its wide spaces.

Braxton Rutledge is not an average sergeant; he is the only black soldier in that particular outpost of the American Army. During the film there is an emphasis on this factor but without making the soldier's presence appear out of place in the eyes of the spectator. For the first time in a western a man of African origin is profiled as the basis of the story. Had the sergeant been of European descent the movie wouldn't have had the same significance. This episode is enlightening because it exposes a drama of our era with powerful images–a humanity predisposed to prejudice against someone who is different. The film doesn't limit itself to pointing out the racial theme within a new context–it also delves into the feelings of men who passionately search for the truth, and when they find it, know how to accept it as a discovery that goes beyond their interests. The movie is an acknowledgement of those who are romantic and are willing to sacrifice themselves for justice rather than conforming. The ability this director has to transmit his own passion to the characters he creates is what sublimates his work. During the storyline it is as if Sergeant Rutledge himself were narrating his experience to us. Maybe it is because John Ford knows that the truth will always remain elusive in his work that he tries to be impartial with the events and wants to give everyone the opportunity to express themselves.

The film is framed within a civil-military setting, between the patrols of the cavalry and the interiors of the courtroom. But the prejudices and the search for the truth turn out to be the real protagonists. The story of Sergeant Rutledge is a summary and almost a premonition of the conflict our society would soon have to face in integration. The drama takes place in a setting well known by aficionados of the American western. During the time of the story, the West was inhabited by people of two cultures with considerably different understandings of the significance of territoriality. The consequences of the war over secession slowly brought another ethnic element into those territories, in the form of the emancipated. Rutledge is a professional soldier who falls into this last category. The main objective of the army in those outposts is to provide security to the people under their protection and to bring calm to areas in conflict. In the zones of greater risk to the colonies, the soldiers where entrusted with protecting the white population. The sergeant was one of these men, satisfied with carrying out the orders of his superiors in the regiment in which he served, and with a disciplined disposition he managed to maintain a clean record of service. Suddenly, a damaging accusation designed to cover up the crime committed by another is made against Rutledge. The soldier is suspected of a crime that is unusual by its very nature and the circumstances in which it takes place. A society without the experience of integration must face an investigation of a crime in which the indicted is of a different color than everyone else in the community. In those territories where the cavalry was making life habitable for white settlers, justice must have been exerted with all the limitations we can imagine. The investigation practices were probably rudimentary, procedures dealt with quickly, and frequently tribunals were presided over by makeshift judges. Sometimes in the absence of a jury, the sentence was handed down by the sheriff, whom circumstances had forced into accelerating the resolution of justice. Trapped by these less-than-favorable conditions, the possibilities of the sergeant escaping the situations alive was unlikely. Fortunately for the accused, the army demanded more guarantees for one of its own. The High Command required deliberation prior to passing sentence, and in the end the black sergeant is saved from great punishment. This is a film by an optimistic man: John Ford decides that an honest conscience will have the necessary energy to go in search of justice where needed and predicts that in the depths of free thought there will always be the required courage to face the truth. During his long career as director he consistently treated the military life with respect, and whenever his camera focused on it, he appeared to want to tell us that in the hearts of good soldiers there is a hospitable space where honor will always have a safe haven.

A dilemma affects the civilian sector of the population, the honor of the Army and its mission that unfolds beyond the sergeant. The repulsive crime infuriated the citizenry, but as the accused is a member of the military, the inhabitants of the colony are forced to surrender the trial to the dictates of a court martial. Even so, the procedure against the sergeant presents an uncomfortable situation that, while avoiding complications whenever possible, requires rapid resolution. It would have been much easier and less disturbing to sacrifice the soldier, but the participants in the process realize the responsibility that weighs on them and understand how important it is for everyone's future to search for the true perpetrator regardless of the consequences. At the beginning it looks as though the trial will have an easy outcome, and everyone expects exemplar punishment for Rutledge when the military tribunal (even an open and fairly casual one) is charged with evaluating the evidence and passing a sentence. A court martial would certainly be more disciplined and demanding in the details than the improvised civil tribunals of the time. Even so, there was the possibility that the unpredictable and frequent tours of the cavalry might precipitate a decision from the jury. Ignoring the prejudices of the settlers, the highest ranks of the military outpost carry out their task with notable impartiality. When the sergeant's innocence comes to light, the guilt of a respected member of the community is discovered, and this convulses the social structures of the colony to its foundations and raises far-reaching complications for the feelings of each of those present. The scandalous court case and its dramatic outcome summon the integrity of the population that serenely responds to the verdict of the jury. The firm conviction of Lieutenant Tom Contrell, who began a crusade to save the life of an innocent man, has a just result. Thanks to the determination of the young official the truth comes out, restoring the honor of Sergeant Rutledge and assuring his freedom. It was the moment to be just and submit to the principles of a civilization that was trying to make its way west. Searching for the truth beyond appearances, gives confidence to their colonization cause. Only those who remain loyal to their convictions deserve the land they inhabit.

History sometimes conceals what the speculations of a free mind discovers or that which on occasion comes to light through the fantasy of an artist. The former is usually a product of a patient and detailed investigation, while the latter is more instinctivel and intuitive than anything else. All works of art reflect the feelings of their author, and are a document of their time, relevant in the manner for which they approach the subject or innocuous for their adaptation of superficial conventionalisms. The work of the artist directly affects our sensibility without it first being evaluated by reason. If this intense communication takes place, art infuses our ethics with the passion they require, and, afterwards, it will be our choice to find the conclusions. Cinema is a manifestation of art in which the ethical and aesthetic impact reach the spectator at the same time, so that reflection on both notions must also be done simultaneously. The simplest stories by the masters of cinematography leave in us an emotional trace that invites us to relive them and ponder their significance. A movie that fails to make us think and doesn't stimulate our imagination, in some sense is not worthy of watching. Movies bring us surprising situations and transport us to places we have never been, entertain the idle viewer with engaging or insignificant episodes, and can also engage our curiosity of history. This film shows us how the struggle between different races might have been in that countryside, and it is an example of art as a catalyst for out interest in the past. In this case, in addition to being a passionate declaration of guilt, this story by Ford contributes to understanding the road this country has traveled during its precarious integration. With modesty and no assurances, Ford attempts to come close to the truth, and it doesn't matter if some of the events have been altered or if this episode is only a product of his imagination. In searching for the truth, the author must make his fantasy a reality, because even though he knows that art tends to be indifferent with regard to questions of conscience, creativity cannot be put at the service of a lie without degrading itself.

Someone must know if this episode of the American cavalry is based on a historic event, as is the case with many other John Ford films. Even so, the situations and scenes that reach the spectator with so much intensity must be the product of the creator's imagination. The director of the movie is not obligated to overly adhere to the text. Whoever attempts to create something original cannot surrender to the dictates of another author and should only commit to his own work. In film it is imperative that the plot have an objective and the narrative have coherence. History is indifferent to the purposes of art. As an ideal it only needs to adjust to the truth. Even so, the tragic destiny of reality becomes a victim to agendas or maliciousness, and many times falsehoods replace the truth. For art's purposes both myth and history are indistinguishably useful without requiring the artist to rigorously adhere to the dictates of the inventor of symbols or the historian. Art impartially contemplates the events of the past and distrusts the intentions of fate but arrogantly feels it has the right to imagine the future and in certain occasions, even corrects history. All that a movie director needs to make a realistic film is for the story to make sense and for that he must liberate himself from the dictates of the text. As history has demonstrated, it can be an insuperable humorist plagued by contradictions and nonsense. Here are some examples. Instead of contributing to disseminate the sermons of Mohammed, the invasion of the south of the Iberian peninsula by the Moslems brings about the expansion of Christianity throughout all of continental Europe. Later on, the Turks have no idea that by closing Europe's passage to the Orient they accelerated the discovery of America while also losing the opportunity to integrate themselves into Western progress. The Inquisition accused those who participated in the more primitive pagan ceremonies of cruelty and, to demonstrate their Christian charity, condemned them to be burned at the stake with green timber. From the liberating ideas of the French Revolution come Napoleon's tyranny; even so, French citizens are proud of both and celebrate the two events with equal enthusiasm. But that is not all. They act as if this contradiction should be an inspiration to the rest. A new theory, with scientific pretensions, emerges and expands across the world at the start of the twentieth century. In spite of its compassionate appearance, this doctrine that proclaims economical equality for all with no social distinctions shows its perverse tendencies, and communism materializes as a heartless bureaucratic farce. Ironically associated with religion, the anti-Semitic persecutions of the past two centuries that denied a country to a race prompted, more than anything else, the creation of the modern state of Israel. Meanwhile, for almost three years the world is horrified by the spectacle of the First World War. After it ended, with the purpose of putting an end to German expansionism and assuring a lasting peace, the allies generate the Treaty of Versailles that brings about an even more terrible war. It appears nearly impossible to tell where a predetermined purpose will end up taking us. Sometimes we end up in a place we had no desire to see, and in the end nobody is completely sure for whom he works or to what cause he is contributing.

History tracks dates, points out memorable moments, and sometimes assigns them exaggerated significance. We continue celebrating every year until myth is defeated and replaced by dogmatic lies, as though the triumph of our civilization depends on it. Following this belief, for centuries the arrival of Christian dogma in all its manifestations is remembered with fervor and devotion, even though this event submerged Europe in darkness for more than a millennium. Taking liberties with historical text does not necessarily imply a lack of truth, but perhaps could be considered a search for the true significance of history. In the brilliant distinction made by Joseph Campbell between reality, myth, and falsehoods, the difference in intention between these concepts is very clear. This American historian also warns of the danger in confusing them and in instituting any of these three notions as an article of faith. The discrepancies that might occur between *Sergeant Rutledge* and the document from which the idea might have been extracted will never be as scandalous as the contradiction that exists between those who proclaim love for fellow beings and human solidarity, while at the same time being proficient in the old book that degrades women, glorifies the attempt to kill your own son, and foments slavery. Aside from the small degree of loyalty that it owes to history, cinema is obligated to be something more congruent and less distanced from the truth. As an example of the compromise that art has had to make in coping with religious pessimism, *Sergeant Rutledge* is part of a humanistic current that tries to give our journey on this planet some meaning.

An event in real life and the representation of it are subjected to individual interpretation. Knowledge of the event incites us to investigate the cause and our curiosity opens a door to speculation. An effort must be made to give it some foundation. *Sergeant Rutledge* appears as part of the work of someone we already know and who has left the imprint of his convictions in us. The film cannot have the same significance for someone who is unaware of the body of work of the director and who wants to evaluate the movie independently. If his religiousness had prevailed in John Ford's Christian development, the conscious dilemmas presented in his films would have a different connotation and the outcome would probably be predictable from the start of the movie. Religion might not be of much use, but at least it doesn't doubt and it establishes a clear line between good and evil. As an extreme opposite to this moral certainty, the work of this director is characterized by the inclusion of conflicting points of view and positions that are treated with respect and understanding. A passionate observer, Ford is not indifferent when presenting his convictions, but he also wants to be fair and let the principles and concerns of the characters be freely represented by the protagonists. In *Sergeant Rutledge* he confronts the racial theme with serenity, without ostentation or cheap condescension and becomes an echo of the European agnosticism that repudiates two centuries of the monstrous practices of slavery (which the Bible legitimizes). Even though some find a moral guide for humanity in the biblical text, this book has been useful to all sects for condemning the descendents of one of the sons of Noah to slavery and distinguishing them with a darker skin. The origin of the notion that made the trafficking of slaves legal is found in religion, even though we are all responsible in some measure for the suffering of each human being. The more culpable try to revise history and cover up the evidence of their injustices while attempting to elude responsibility by adjusting the course of events to their doctrine. To do this they have given confusing definitions to certain terms. In contrast, Greek reflection was able to contemplate the cosmos without interference from dogma and, while in search of the truth, speculate on concepts and ideas—not on terminology that remains unalterable. Their heirs, the Romans, begin to modify the meaning of words and bring about the birth of rhetoric and as a consequence Europe is introduced to Christianity. Considerably prior to the proclamation of the monotheist doctrine as absolute truth, discourse and moral teachings in Greece had given humanity the freedom for analysis and responsibility for their behavior with others and within their own conscience. Compared to the immense ethical contribution of classical culture, Oriental messianism has only come up with ten unappealable laws and imaginary punishment. The differences between these two proposals have been continuously manifested through the millenniums and each has its innumerable supporters. But from time immemorial until now, Western civilization has been the only one with the sufficient humility to recognize its own faults and assert its blame. This film is one such example.

The Man Who Shot Liberty Valance - 1962

> Ramson Stodard garners fame and becomes a
> senator in recognition of slaying the dangerous
> Liberty Valance, but in reality it was his friend
> Tom Doniphon who saved his life and did away
> with the criminal. For years Tom strives to make
> people see in Stodard the man that should represent
> them in the Senate in Washington.

The flashback is not the most captivating technique used in film, but it is the most effective way of separating two periods of time in the mind of the spectator. The reason for this is that it allows the contemplation of the story through the thoughts of the person recording it. It can be disturbing sometimes, because it forces us to follow the development of the narrative from afar. When it is necessary to establish chronological distances, the reproduction of scenes based on memories helps the director maintain the rhythm of the movie and give sense to the story. In *How Green Was My Valley*, where time is also a protagonist, John Ford uses the memories of one of the characters to clearly distinguish the space between two different times and give greater sentimental impact to the movie. In *The Man Who Shot Liberty Valance*, time is part of the story and becomes an allegory in the film. It is what determines the validity of the three paths that each of the protagonists symbolizes. Liberty Valance, representing the past, must be eliminated by Doniphon, who is firmly situated in the present and facilitates the arrival of the future Senator Stoddard. The latter also represents the law, to be imposed on the last vestige of the savage and anarchic Wild West–the fall of which we watch with so much nostalgia and sympathy. Valance, fierce and arbitrary, doesn't see much room for himself in the coming order of things, nor is he interested in forming part of a society where his licentious image will be immediately rejected. He realizes that soon those who share the hopes of Ransom Stoddard will consider him subversive. The outlaw, in spite of his aggressiveness, is more of a romantic figure than those who will inevitably replace him–undoubtedly much more acceptable but less engaging personalities. His tragedy is that of those condemned to failure, and his disappearance moves us, as his exit represents the end of a colorful era.

The quality of a movie depends on the value it gives to the human beings in it, the fidelity with which it reproduces its surroundings, and the respect that the director shows towards these two components. The imagination of the director is also conditioned by the circumstances that limit the action of the characters and in his role as conductor, he is forced to contemplate the world through them. Ford assigns to one of the protagonists the task of evoking the past. When Senator Ransom Stoddard returns to Shinbone to attend the funeral of his friend Tom Doniphon, he allows his memories to flow freely, bringing us the story through his recollections. But this film is better seen through the eyes of Liberty Valance. For those who did not perceive the humor in this tragic character, years later, under the direction of Elliot Silverstein in *Cat Ballou*, this actor constructs a more obvious version of the irony found in his misfortune following the Civil War. The taming of the West produced the dangerous explorer who spread throughout the continent. This archetype adapts his behavior to become the individualistic and nomadic hero whose nobility was made legendary in film. The horse gave his image elegance, and the railroad provided him with more dynamism. But in the end, the automobile converted him into an anachronistic figure and displaced him. Technology established its standards and, before anyone noticed, Dillinger had replaced Jesse James. Foreseeing this process, Liberty Valance instantly loathes Ransom Stoddard because he sees in him the ominous change that will replace him. He detests Stoddard's manners on sight and scorns his set of values, which do not fit the world he has inhabited until then. He feels incapable of adjusting to the outlook that the future Senator forecasts. It irritates Valance that Doniphon–whom he fears but recognizes as someone from his own class–defends the intruder who has come to replace them both. The confrontation between these two is one of the most delicious exchanges ever shown on screen.

It is Ford's tendency to refer us constantly to the drama of eras in the process of extinction and to project images in the process of disappearing. In the unlikely event that he might have wished to do a prehistoric chronicle, the character he most probably would have selected would have represented the nomadic hunter who, with the arrival of agriculture, becomes obsolete to the needs of the tribe, and who sees his social stature diminishing. Had he ever decided to cover the classical period of history, it is unlikely that he would have chosen to make a film about the splendor of Greek civilization. He would have been much more attracted to narrating its fall. If he had chosen a troubadour as the hero of his film, he would have placed him at the time when the enthusiasm for his songs is diminishing and his verses are no longer required in the medieval castles. One of the films John Ford must have felt a great affinity for is *Lonely Are The Brave* by David Miller, where the last cowboy dies in the street; his career ending under the wheels of a truck. This unconscious tendency to observe the romantic aspects of life is born from a substantially rational tradition and does not adapt to the conventionalities driven by a belief in providence. The certain and dogmatic doctrine flee from what is genuine and is not compatible with the individual attitudes of those willing to sacrifice themselves, even if they have no hope of a reward. Even though during the course of Ford's movies there might be a

ceremony or temple, these scenes are never intended as a religious affirmation, nor do they suggest the notion of the supernatural. He does not resort–as some directors–to extravagances that could dislodge the characters from their earthly condition. He also didn't experiment with fantastic subjects in the style of *2001: A Space Odyssey* by Stanley Kubrick, which has the appearance of invoking forces superior to those of the universe. In contrast, Ford's cinema is firmly situated on earth, in the deep relationship with nature and above all, concerning the incorruptible human subject. If his films had to be described in two words, perhaps it would be "romantic realism."

The intention of the director is to communicate to us a simple fragment of history. But the subconscious impels him to interpret history according to the same standards that have shaped his character. Within the same mind, it is impossible to reconcile superstition with logic or reason. The artist must decide on one of these two paths, which will reveal his inclinations. Those adept at providence will claim to be in possession of the truth, although they do not demonstrate even the smallest amount of interest in it. They deform and degrade truth without understanding it. The more romantic spirits run in search of the truth, without any certainty of ever finding that desirable yet elusive lady. Since antiquity, they have created terms that clarified concepts and that we continue to employ today. The others introduced words with the intention of confusing and mystifying ideas. Not all ethnic groups have demonstrated the same disposition or ability to have these two tendencies coexist. Western man almost resolves this dilemma by finding a different mental space for each of these contradictory positions, creating a society where dogma is only a routine and barely an obstacle to the development of scientific investigation and the free expression of the artist. No one has been able to completely remove the influence of either of these two positions, but one of them will remain in the mind of the artist and will be reflected in his creations. To a certain extent, the work reveals the subconscious of its creator. Intentionally or not, each image has significance and a certain symbolism both for the creator as well as the viewer. In cinematic mythology, a desperate Liberty Valance is a hopeless and violent pagan protest against the passage of time.

Religion comes from man's fantasy; it feeds from the belief in the supernatural and defends its principles through sophistry. Science can only happen through free analysis and reasoning. Aesthetics, unconcerned with ethical aspects, can freely choose any direction as long as the work remains consistent to the chosen path. The pagan condition of art faced centuries of persecution, but has never been completely suppressed, not even during the times of greater intolerance. It springs from man's subconscious just as plants do in the desert when water makes the most minimal contact. This disposition frees the most primitive impulses of man but also brings forth the best that dwells inside. To represent the romantic vocation of the hero, the catalyst of our ideals, is a bit of a poetic feat. For the author, the path is easier when he deeply identifies with the principles of his own culture. The work of John Ford is one of the most revealing representations of Western civilization portrayed in art during the entire twentieth century. His free and fatalist disposition is demonstrated once again in *The Man Who Shot Liberty*

Valance. His irreverent intentions are most evident in the church scene when the character enters the place of worship on horseback during a political gathering. The American background of this film is also unmistakable in the subject that it covers and in its development. Situations happen as circumstances dictate, and so does the outcome. The one with the most probability of surviving does just that. Nothing is left to providence.

The Man Who Shot Liberty Valance is a work born from the agnostic perception of history. It speaks to us of time, the way human beings adjust to it and change its appearance. The protagonists are perfectly defined. There isn't any confusion as to what each represents. Everything is clear and constructed for us to follow the development of the film without forcing ourselves to distinguish the nuances of the conflict. Even though the characters profess to be believers, their behavior does not appear to be influenced by religion. The director didn't need to return to Christian morality to explain their actions. It is time not the seminary that changes the conditions of their lives, that motivates them to act. The symbols of the movie are the three gods of chronology: past, present, and future. These three representations have nothing biblical about them. Tom Doniphon, the hero of this trilogy, is also the personification of the politics of the moment, when he decides who is to survive. He is a man who lives in the present, but knows the past and feels the need to sacrifice it for the benefit of the future. Everything that happens is the result of these factors impacting the events being shown. Senator Stoddard is aware how things are and how easily they could have turned out differently. It isn't possible to assure the future of our existence, but we can be sure that no one can halt the passage of time.

The Cheyenne Autumn – 1964

> The exodus of the Cheyenne tribe in all its misery,
> while enduring a particularly fierce autumn for
> over a thousand miles. Everything is collective: the
> incomprehension, the government's idleness, and
> the heroic death of those who dared rebel. In the
> end the tribe disperses after Little Wolf is forced to
> kill Red Shirt.

The journey of the American family towards the opposite coast was a prolonged adventure that offered limitless topics to be used by literature and the cinematographer. The progress of that enormous relocation that lasted more than a century had moments of glory. Throughout its course there were heroic deeds, but the suffering of its victims was frequently ignored. From the beginning, Hollywood has nurtured itself from the considerable variety of situations that this race to the West offered the imagination. Nonetheless, a historic account without the human touch to give it life was usually sterile and boring, and the very first producers understood that in order to get their plans started and make way for the new industry, cinema needed to rely on the ingeniousness of the writer and the fantasy of the artist. The talent of these originators was immediately taken advantage of by the budding film activity. In a short period of time, in a stampede that was somewhat less than that of the previous century yet still considerable, a portion of the planet's creative sector migrated to this placid western point of the continent. Initially they concentrated their cameras on the absurdities of human behavior that offer so many possibilities for comedy. Afterwards their attention spread to a landscape close by, which was being quickly transformed. They observed it by going back a few decades in time and adjusting the course of history to their commercial purposes. That is how the cowboy and the Indian spawned a whole cinematic genre, which didn't yet have a name but was destined to flourish. Arriving from the East along with many others, John Ford was on hand in the movie capital during the early days of the western. As an actor and director during his early years in the studios, Ford had the opportunity to contribute to the benefits quickly garnered by others in the trivialization of American West history, often reducing it to a series of entertaining and inconsequential episodes. Early on those movies had been crafted for viewers who identified with the characters portrayed, and consequently the producers made sure the heroes of these films shared the purposes and aspirations of the public. Hollywood was minimizing recent history and, perhaps without meaning to, John Ford's discerning ability gradually led him to investigate the consequences of these confrontations that early cinema overlooked. In each movie, he gradually incorporated the conflictive aspects of the clash of cultures into his westerns, trying to be impartial and justifying events based on the circumstances. Committed to his ethical principles, he felt that, in the expressionistic realism of his work, the image of those most in need of justice was being sacrificed. From then on, he tried to include the opinions of those who had lost it all. In one movie after another, through historical documents and experiences, he introduced his discoveries that the silver screen had rejected until then. After participating for more than a decade in the production of movies of indistinguishable stories, Ford felt the innate curiosity for the past which steered him to research the actual events of western expansion. In the end, with the debut of *The Cheyenne Autumn*, the director made a historical declaration of culpability that affects us all.

John Ford sacrificed his inclination to admire the individual in order to better represent the Cheyenne spirit and make the entire population a protagonist in his story. He travels back in time to that raw autumn to understand them better because he wanted to learn more about the tragedy of an entire race. With reverence he formulates questions, transmitting to us the results of his investigation. He subtly alters the public perception so that after witnessing this accusatory condemnation, the viewers will be more capable of understanding the feelings and experiences of the protagonists. Compassionate towards both sides in his observations, Ford leaves no doubt as to the value of the two fighting settlements. He praises the courage of the pioneer and the asceticism of his spirit of adventure, but does not tolerate any attempts against the dignity of the defeated. In this film, the last of the Cheyenne are the representatives of this culture of the plains, symbols of the bravery of the tribes that circulated those vast spaces and an allegory of all the people who, even in their final agony, kept their honor intact. John Ford intended this film to indicate a change in the history of Hollywood. His passionate indictment is in support of the Indians. They are the reason for this movie and the substance of the dramatic narrative. Compared to the magnitude of the Cheyenne exodus, he makes Thomas Archer–who should be the main protagonist–into a simple messenger, a marginal and opaque character. Forty years earlier, with equal passion he had praised the march of America to its frontiers in *The Iron Horse*, telling the tale of the most devastating instrument to be faced by a nomadic culture. *The Cheyenne Autumn* is homage to the memory of a culture that we caused to disappear, and a personal tribute dedicated to those whose nobility awakened our feelings of solidarity.

The nation's registries have gathered the testimonies written in Cheyenne blood and from the cold archives of the Secretary of the Interior Ford rescued the document that appeared to interest no one–and in this manner produced one of his most moving films. The author of this movie burrowed through history in search of details that give substance to his chronicle, investigated the abuse that incomprehension and indifference precipitated, and obtained one more piece of evidence of the bureaucratic insensibility that began by first offending the dignity of a tribe, and finally pushing it to extinction. John Ford was scrupulous with the essence of the story, and when he traveled from Hollywood to Monument Valley to direct *The Cheyenne Autumn*, one of the trucks was loaded with books for consultation. The respect with which the tragic sacrifice of these people is portrayed has a painful realism because the author understood the tragedy to its very roots. In order to exalt the image of its heroes and give recognition to the risky achievement that America carried out in establishing the limits of its frontiers, history has sometimes forgotten the suffering of those who were sacrificed on the way. Ford decided to remedy this unfair omission. As a confidant of the heirs of the Cheyenne tribe, he became a passionate chronicler of their misadventures. With equanimity, he wanted to redeem those who had no voice in history and announce that this chapter would be narrated taking into account the feelings and the ordeal of the victims. He imposed upon himself the obligation to relive that sad episode in a truthful manner, and without resentment he makes ignorance, as cruel as it can sometimes be, responsible for the massacre. The director's interest to make known the reasons for the sacrifice of those people led him to detail the exodus of the Cheyenne while avoiding the path to artificial benevolence. In the historic document, Ford found evidence that confirmed the details of the disastrous relocation, and in the end he only asks for recognition of their noble existence. Ford said that this time he wanted to be their voice in their agonizing fall. He accepts that responsibility for every American, and using the evacuation of a people in distress like an alchemist of the imagination, he makes his thoughts our conscience.

The director begins his story when history already indicates the final destiny of the Indo-American cultures. The foundations that sustained the life of the indigenous have been ruined by the arrival of civilization and the future offered an apocalyptic panorama for the natives of this country. The white man arrogantly proclaims himself owner of the territories upon which he has settled. The fields shall provide sustenance for his cattle, and the products from the earth belong to only him. The new inhabitant of the plains has methods at his disposal that allow him to ignore the effects of the climate, and he doesn't follow nature's dictates. He sometimes makes adjustments for it, other times he defies it, but the seasons do not determine his conduct. Accustomed to these advantages he cannot comprehend the importance the nomadic trips represent to the existence of the Indians, following the sun just like the flocks of migrating birds and droves that accompany them. Herds of roaming buffalo crash into the white man's barbed wire that squares off the land, also disrupting the passage of the tribes that need to keep pace with the animals. The new sovereigns are not gods but imposters, mortal beings that do not respect their customs nor recognize their culture. They have brought noisy weapons that spit fire and now, as a formidable and ominous monster, the iron horse that roars across the landscape, interrupting the millenary cycle of indigenous migrations. Lastly, without knowing why, they are denied unrestricted passage across lands that belong to everyone–just as the wind, the moon, the sun, and the stars in the sky belong to everyone. Breaking the laws of the land, the intruders from afar believe they have the right to force the Cheyenne people to migrate in the opposite direction than what the climate dictates. Accepting his impotence, Chief Dull Knife announces that this autumn the migration will take place in the other direction. Forced to move in the opposite direction to the cycle that they had followed for hundreds of years, he guides his people on what will be a journey without hope. By design of the intruder, the Indians will go against the stars in their passage, and these will make sure that nature will go against them. What was once in their favor will turn hostile, and suddenly the equinoxes and the solstices will no longer be favorable. It is as if the universe has gone mad. Abandoned by their gods, they search for something that will respond to their anguished uncertainty.

These are two conflicting worlds and two opposing perceptions of the cosmos in confrontation. On one hand, Western culture, a supporter of progress, arrives in the new world influenced by the unifying element of faith that gives it strength and makes it unconscious of the feelings of those who do not share their beliefs. In contrast, the indigenous pantheism is not belligerent, lacks a unifying objective, tends toward freedom, and tolerates outside ways of life at a distance. The morals of the white people are dictated by an invisible entity that, in spite of his impalpable absence, has been proclaimed superior by the new neighbors to all of the natural phenomena present every day. Long experience has shown Chief Dull Knife that it will be useless to appeal to the comprehension of those who feel themselves in possession of the truth and owners of the land. Since he was a child

he has seen the pale faces increase in number and strength, while at the same time white man's insensibility has decimated the population of other tribes. The chief knows that the destiny of integration will leave little of his culture but might provide some future for the youngest of his race. This is his only hope, because there is no other way to continue fighting. The Indian chief and the white teacher who accompanies them are the only ones who truly understand this unavoidable reality, and she is confident in a more promising future for those who are not yet of an age to understand the magnitude of their misfortune. The calamity has also divided the tribe with debates between cultural permanence and the physical survival of the last Cheyenne. In the course of the journey, during winter and without protection against the elements, the compassionate pragmatism of Dull Knife clashes against the belligerent determination of Red Shirt. The chief must sacrifice his pride to maintain the unity of those who are left, but it will all be in vain. Little Wolf is forced to kill the rebel and, with his blood on his hands, Wolf must leave without hope. With immeasurable and resigned desperation, Dull Knife appears to reflect upon how this once proud and audacious people are now without future and at the mercy of others, about to be defeated by history. A sad destiny for a proud and free nation.

In a different way, the teacher, Deborah Wright, also experiences the helplessness of the Cheyenne, and her maternal instincts have led her to concentrate her selfless labor towards the youngest of the tribe. She has lived with the Indians, and thanks to them she realizes that the laws of the land only respond in favor to those who obey them. She has also witnessed how decisions made by the white man reduce the physical resistance of the Indians: Disease and famine have reduced the number of survivors to less than three hundred. Indifferent functionaries make decrees and give orders from afar that have an effect on nameless men and women, inhabitants of the topography, and victimized by a climate the bureaucrats do not take into account. She can fully understand the significance of this tragedy and manages to encourage Captain Thomas Archer to intercede on behalf of these long-suffering people. The intentions of the Secretary of the Interior do not consider in any way the necessities of what is left of that tribe. The intention of the orders is to assure that the existence of the Indians will not cause any more inconveniences. Those in their offices, who for years made decisions, could never envision what the sensibility of John Ford would perceive almost instantly a century later. With their bureaucratic ignorance they committed what in politics is considered something worse than a crime: a mistake. John Ford places the failure and unscrupulousness in Washington, and the offhand manner of the white man towards the Indians in Dodge City, where the heroes of another of his movies appear swathed in a life of prosperity and licentiousness. Like a conjurer, he pulls Wyatt Earp and Doc Holliday from his repertoire and presents them impromptu on a cheerful bender. This group of carefree and happy citizens almost crosses paths during their orgiastic excursion with the discouraged and starving caravan, without the silent misfortune of the Indians quite reaching them. In contrast to the amusing excess of abundance, the Cheyenne take flight in search of freedom, finding only misery, bitter cold, and eventually isolation and death. The sequences in the film belong to a composed stage design, but the realism of the images causes a sensation similar to the emotional African photographs of Leni Riefenstahl. John Ford wanted to give the Indians a voice in history, paying a debt of honor that belongs to each of us. He does something else: Ford raises our consciousness so that with this single episode we will better understand the meaning of our American past.

Seven Women – 1966

> In 1935 a religious mission in China is attacked
> and the women are kidnapped by bandits. Moved
> by their situation and the future of the newborn
> child, Dr. D.C. Cartwright sacrifices her life to
> save them.

Doctrines have power to unite people, but they also stimulate fanaticism and
aid the ecclesiastical hierarchy by making the population into a frequently
violent instrument of religious diffusion. The Christian missions, however with
much more conciliatory methods, compel the same proselytizing objective. The
pacifist function of the missions does not imply that this is an activity exempt
from danger. On the contrary, on occasions evangelical work can result in
heroics. Missionaries in general prefer to preach among populations under
great hardship and address groups that have little access to cultural knowledge.
Misery, hunger, and pestilence offer splendid opportunities to spread doctrines
within less-enlightened communities. Under similar pitiful circumstances,
Agatha Andrews lead a congregation in a remote part of China, spreading
evangelism and trying to attract parishioners to her faith. A rampant epidemic
in that area kept the mission quite active during 1935 when, suddenly, the seven
women are captured by bandits under the orders of Tunga Khan. The situation
becomes even more dismal when one of them gives birth in the infested prison.
As a consequence of this unforeseen event, from the resigned outlook of the
group surges the maternal instinct. They immediately adapt to the
circumstances, but the submissive passivity of the women is transformed by the
appearance of Dr. Cartwright. With her arrival comes scientific reason, able to
observe nature free from prejudices and at odds with the religious dispositions
of the other women. The doctor sees the birth of the child as an image of life,
and out of solidarity for her new companions she feels the need to do
something for the seven women and the newborn. After recognizing the
situation and the miserable confinement of the missionaries, Cartwright is
compelled to mediate with Tunga on their behalf. From that moment on, each
of these three characters of this tragedy becomes a symbol of their respective

backgrounds and convictions. What to Tunga signifies strength, to Cartwright is biology (and to Andrews everything is reduced to religion). When the issue of morality comes up, the women are soon faced with the difference in appreciation that exists between faith and scientific pragmatism. Sex also makes an appearance, but this time in the role of sacrifice. Dr. Cartwright is a female who understands the meaning of sexuality, which is why her surrender will be that much more painful, although to Miss Andrews her gesture was an offense against Christian orders. It is made evident once again that sex is the only expression of nature that dogma continues to underhandedly manipulate and, for the free individual, it is an instinctive practice that affects the intimacy of our feelings. Both tend to relate eroticism to morality, but one of them is tolerant in this respect while the other is not. It doesn't matter how noble her purposes might be, in the opinion of the supervisor of the mission, the physical submission of Cartwright is unforgivable. Miss Andrews cannot appreciate the heroic actions of the doctor, she doesn't even approve of the generous act committed to save them. The only thing she can perceive in Cartwright's sacrifice is the sin.

Maternity is a biological occurrence; paternity is only its social consequence, which is perhaps why the manifestation of the sexual urge in a woman is less spontaneous and much more circumstantial than in a man. Maybe that is why on occasion it is somewhat difficult for us to understand and even appreciate feminine behavior. There is a magical transmutation in the protective reaction of Cartwright that transcends her scientific manner. She makes her decision rationally but stimulated by the recent birth that has activated her animal instinct as guardian of the species. The maternity of the young missionary Florrie Pether has inspired this selfless gesture, making the doctor the heroine of her sex and the mother of each of the women. The passion that rouses those female instincts responsible for the continuity of the species joins her rational and disciplined scientific attitude. She can be calculating and ferocious, she will destroy the person who holds them prisoner, but she is also willing to surrender her body and her life. Whatever the cost, at any price, by any means and with whatever weapon is needed to fulfill the supreme mission that every woman carries inside: The oppressor lives on borrowed time. Tunga, with his brutish conviction of the law of the strongest, falls dejected at the hands of someone who, with cold serenity, came to understand him better than what he could have imagined. It is possible that in the end, this brutal Chinese man might be able to admire the romantic gesture of the woman who eliminates him. Each of the emblematic characters remains faithful to their convictions: Miss Andrews behaves according to her religious beliefs, Tunga's instincts guide his actions in relation to the power he holds, and Cartwright can only act according to her conscience.

In Ford's cinema the woman has always been the reason behind the efforts of the male, the object of his reverence, and the refuge of the family; she is now also the initiator of the events. The narrative this time is an acknowledgement of the civilizing intentions of our culture and a tribute to the efforts of the woman in this task. The courted female, inspiration to action in other films by this director, is his principle protagonist in this movie. In that remote part of the planet, she is the valiant personification of our identity and our humanism. This movie confirms that the feminine presence has been an essential factor in extending Western influence across frontiers. The dramatic episode that Ford recounts to us is an allegory dedicated to the heroic function of the woman in all of the advances of our civilization. Through Agatha Andrews, the director wants to make an affirmation of his Christian faith, but his Catholicism appears to have an effect solely within the traditional manner–more formal than doctrinarian. John Ford decides to remain absent in the conflict, and he doesn't try to circumvent the triumph of the romantic spirit over the religiousness of Miss Andrews. From a distance and without passing sentence, he lets the events provide the reason for the evident agnosticism of Dr. Cartwright. In spite of his laconic style, he makes clear his inclination for the less religious of the women and manages to make this preference appear well justified. Symbolism in Ford's movies has more than anything a subjective character–never presented in a concrete fashion. It is subtle in *Stagecoach*, *The Searchers*, or *The Man Who Shot Liberty Valance*, and more evident in *The Fugitive* and *Seven Women*, his two films with religious themes. In this, the last great movie by John Ford, each of the women is a representation of many. He defines them in such a way that we recognize in their images the different attitudes adopted by females to survive and protect their offspring under painful conditions. In a distant colony of Asia, the conflict between these women is an indication of the pagan and Christian duality of our society. If they can stay together with these opposite dispositions, it is only to better endure the brutality to which they are being subjected. Weighed down by these circumstances, together they face the social excrescence of the China of that time, where the revolution would begin to impose its dictates within ten years. That change meant the end of that ancient culture, the last years of an old way of life.

John Ford makes the superior qualities of the woman stand out in a hostile environment that is still connected to the ancient society that at least offered some hope. The story has possibilities within the boundaries of China back then. The feminism of the missionaries would have been exterminated or nullified under the totalitarian regime that would eventually take over or in an Islamic territory in the Middle East. Men from Southwest Asia are not accustomed to having women participate in their social life. If the director had decided to place the missionaries in the center of Arabia, the story would have resulted between the comedic and the impossible. In those Moslem enclaves the woman is not a being with free will, but a possession subjected to the wishes of her owner. It isn't necessary to be an anthropological expert to distinguish the different social statuses that women have in the other end of Asia. In Japan, for example, the relationship between a man and a woman is more comparable to our customs than to the practices of Arab countries that are geographically closer to us. Even so, after her arrival in the Far East, the behavior of Western woman must have caused a certain degree of confusion. The free initiative that began to characterize the conduct of European women in the nineteenth century was far from being assimilated by other cultures until after the Second World War. Even when traditionally the Chinese woman was an important part of the family, she did not aspire to the independence of the Europeans or the political power Western culture had conceded to feminism. One of the themes of the movie is the impact caused by the encounter of diverse socio-cultural perspectives and how the varied points of view of each individual can get beyond ethical differences and reconcile at some point. The Christianized Saxon society and the demographic diversity offered by the vast Chinese territory are two not very homogenous worlds that come face to face in this film, which also foments inner conflicts not yet resolved. Their differences in appreciation are amplified by the fact that each of the two cultures is represented by the opposite sex. Their lawless condition and customs direct the actions of the bandits, just as the missionaries will remain contained by the beliefs and norms of the civilization to which they belong. The peculiarity of the encounter and his social alienation determine the behavior of Tunga and his men with relation to the devout, whose conduct is influenced by Christianity, the ethnical heredity that guides their subconscious and the religious norms to which they are conditioned. The seven women are the foundation and the substance of this story, and they are surrounded by the characters that give realism to the movie. This time Woman, in her natural functions as a civilized being, the foundation of the human species, and representative of Western culture, is the essential element in Ford's dialogue.

Through the film, Ford carries out an open defense of his feminist vocation that not everyone was aware of before. This time he wants to give a higher standing to the presence of these women in the Far East, not put them into competition with man. To highlight their symbolism, the director brutalizes the masculine figure to draw a distinction against the resignation of the missionaries. Incisive psychologist, Ford searches for contrasting images and draws particular attention to the delicacy of the woman in disparity to the senseless and coarse attitudes of their opposite sex. The radiant femininity stands out better against the dark background provided by the ominous figure of the leader of the bandits. Maybe that is why he didn't wish to make Tunga into an ordinary Chinese man, who–according to his physical characteristics–appears to be Mongol while his behavior and style do not correspond to the exquisite refinement of the southern Chinese, who tend more towards cruelty than barbarity. In any event, this man does not know how to deal with women on the same terms that a European man does, nor would it occur to him to behave in the manner of an inhabitant from the Arab world. In spite of his ferocity, there is something inherited from the past that allows him to converse with these women and even negotiate with them. The women would have been indiscriminately classified as Gentiles by the inhabitants of the Mediterranean and the Orient. Tunga is the last of his species who in a few years would become part of the march with Mao Tse-Tung and whose personality would be diluted. This metamorphosis would be inevitable. Under the socialist authority Tunga would add rhetoric and hypocrisy to his brutality, developing into a truly repugnant specimen. This had to happen, as the underprivileged are destined to swell the ranks of the new order, since, according to the communist proposals, "discrimination is a bourgeois prejudice that capitalism uses to divide the populace." A bandit with a similar political disposition and missionaries in the service of an authoritarian system would have been useless to any artistic or humanist purpose.

When this movie began production Ford could already see the results of the regime that had established itself twenty years earlier. But most likely, the prospect of considering the new China and possibly updating his story was not very appealing. The events of the story and the images produced would only be believable if placed within the pre-communist society. In the modern China of 1966–now showing its age–the imagination of the director would not have been able to visualize a realistic setting for the conflict, nor would he have been able to make the episodes of this drama credible. To behave as the protagonists, it would be necessary to glimpse the possibility of freedom, and totalitarianism does not allow even a glimmer of free will for the individual. The lenses of Fellini, Welles, or Kurosawa would never penetrate the somber dominions of Communist China either. After the arrival of this nascent bureaucracy, the characters in Ford's movie would be condemned, by the peculiarities of socialism, to never cross paths. Only the parasites of the state and those who would remain docile within its bureaucracy would have a place in the future of that new society. Socialism and fascism go hand in hand, and even when they separate for a moment, they don't delay getting back together. They need each other; just as flowers need bees to reproduce. One promises to satisfy all the demands while the other provides the equipment and methods for the application of the scheme. Related to religion, Marxism is a descendant of the doctrines of the eastern Mediterranean, which had spread through Europe across the old sea two millenniums earlier. More recently, Marxist theories were initially received with enthusiasm, but the solutions they offered were never even put into practice. Socialism has been a disappointing experiment in various continents and has paralyzed progress in the afflicted countries. As for the inefficiency of bureaucratic philanthropy, both theory and empirical study coincide in their conclusions. Even in countries considered capitalist, all nationalized organizations–insurance, public welfare, education, etc.–are more or less inoperative and have a somewhat fraudulent character. The socialist experiment in Europe had catastrophic consequences, but in spite of this, one of those countries is responsible for extending the communist dogma to the Orient. Years later, the Marxist proposal arrived in the Far East so altered that it would have been impossible to divine its original appearance based on its current features. It has failed in all areas and has not contributed in any way to creative activity, and film in particular has decayed miserably wherever Marxist thought has been present. All that is left to see is if the theory can be successfully applied in the theocratic states of Southeast Asia. At least between religion and Marxism there is a shared messianism born from the same source. If this attempt is successful, the doctrine would return to its place of origin and perhaps be useful in effecting a sociological study on the different ethnic dispositions in relation to government. Ford is the antithesis to the social uniformity proposed by this policy. His individualism demands that the actions of the characters remain true to their passions. The realism of the films of this director would also have been weakened if during narration the laws of nature were dictated by some supernatural authority. The essence of his storytelling is always concentrated on the humanism of the protagonists. In *Seven Women* they

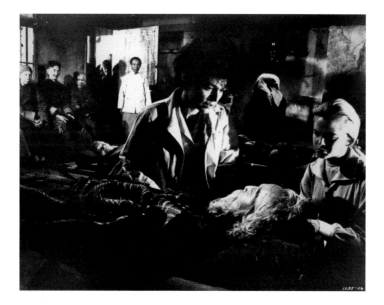

are beings that make an effort to communicate among each other, hoping to overcome their cultural differences, something that would be impossible to attempt under the dictates of a distorted dictatorship.

Ford made numerous movies commissioned by the government during the Second World War, but he never allowed propaganda to invade his field of creative action. In the films he directed there is no favoritism for a particular religion. He only gave value to valiant, selfless, and honest positions, and endeavored that these be in favor of the outcome. The cinema of John Ford is upheld by these profound ethical convictions, and he persisted in referring to human desires and the violent reactions of man as the inescapable consequences of life. In *The Grapes of Wrath* the human behavior of the Joad family and the idealism of union leader Casy are truly touching; the political party to which he belongs isn't even mentioned. While viewing *The Last Hurrah* it is difficult to believe that pragmatic mayor Skeffington favors a particular political tendency. The priest that Ford films in *The Fugitive* and his conflict with conscience is what is important, not the sect to which he belongs. John Ford has confessed to the Catholic roots that underlie his behavior, but without favoring any particular doctrine during the making of his movies. Within these norms, the director realizes a vigorous affirmation of feminism and liberty through *Seven Women*. The Christian orthodoxy of Miss Andrews does not obtain the support of the viewer in this movie. On the contrary, the judgment of the public is for the irreverent conduct of Dr. Cartwright. There is a certain contradiction between realism and piety that as a movie director John Ford decided to take very much into account, setting aside his religious affiliation when he is about to film a scene. As far as this aspect is concerned, he preferred to remain completely impartial. While behind a camera, his analytical position is similar to that of the wise man who asserted that, upon entering the laboratory, he would hang his beliefs on a hook, along with his jacket. Similar to the conscientious scientific investigator, he places before our eyes everything he discovers on human nature, even if what he finds contradicts the fundamentals of his faith. John Ford confirms that his Christianity impels him to distance himself from violence, and his convictions do not allow him to display unnecessary sexual exhibitionism. Even so, both violence and sex are implicit in the moving realism of *Seven Women*. The scene chosen by this director to culminate the film is a disturbing moment of lewdness and death that collides with the religious principles he professes.

For a story to deserve the description of realistic there is no alternative; sex and violence must make an appearance somewhere. The first as a stimulant to the survival of the species and violence as the inevitable activity of each individual in his struggle to survive. Even in its most civilized state, humanity has not been able to refrain from the aggressive tendency of survival. In our society, violence is manifested in a spontaneous way, among individuals defending their belongings or when according to the geopolitical interests of governments, when countries methodically organize themselves for war. Religion has tried to conceal the violent destiny of life, introducing absurd ideas into our thinking and distancing man from contact with nature. Scientific investigation has put into evidence this deception and, in doing so, has caused irreconcilable differences between knowledge and dogma. To relate to this now we must first reflect that the perceptions of an observer of both notions will have varied dramatically during the past century. Influenced by the social changes brought about by science, latter generations are accustomed to contemplating life with a different disposition than their elders. Sex no longer has the same veiled meaning for us, and extraterrestrial life is perceived closer to science-fiction than to providence. Cinema is born and develops during this process of conceptual revolution that technology has and continues to favor.

John Ford lived through a period where the greatest changes in the conscience of humanity have taken place, and by the time he left, the man was no longer the same one we knew during the early years of the film industry. In the course of his existence more innovations have been made than during any other period of history. Since prehistoric times, the human mind had not received such impact. Just as magic's prestige must have diminished when the earth's inhabitants discovered their ability to make fire, in the same respect with the disintegration of the atom, God's image pales in the light of the uncontrollable powers of science. These two impressive milestones of humanity's existence have altered the cosmography of man. Through the immensity of time, by becoming conscious of his power, humanity's perceptions have been altered and, with it, there has been a modification of concepts. After the disturbing ecological and nuclear experience of the twentieth century, Redemption and the Apocalypse no longer have the same divine connotation. We have changed the landscape and broadened our space. The universe continues to be as unknown as always, but by defying gravity we have begun to explore it; everything appears to be in our hands. In the religious context, faith loses ground to the skeptical and nihilist thinking that dominates the intellectual panorama of politics. It is possible that by abandoning dogma we are on our way back to Greece. That would be the end of a deception, as religion is not European in origin but through repetition, its messengers attempted to persuade us that within it could be found the beginning of our civilization. As far as we now know, dogmatism originated in Asia Minor and paralyzed everything upon its arrival in Europe. Western civilization began in Greece, regardless of how impregnated with Christianity it might be now. The thirst for knowledge and, with it, rationality and analytic thinking also developed and prospered on the European continent. To our civilization, everything east of Athens is the Orient, in philosophy, art, and history. Those who have inherited the Western culture and understand its significance can only be Christian in a rhetorical manner. The conflicts in the narrative by Ford surge from the duality found in our norms of conduct: On one hand we have individualism, romantic and daring; on the other a providential and utilitarian religiosity. With *Seven Women* the Occidental soul arrives in China falsely represented by a religious mission, while Dr. Cartwright corrects this imposture by offering scientific advances to those who need them. Afterwards, by making her sacrifice an instrument of freedom, she becomes a romantic symbol of our culture.

The movie is a monumental homage to the woman sublimated by a sentimental man, which is to say that *Seven Women* reflects the emotion felt by the director for the captivating enchantment of the stoic female sacrifice in benefit of the continuity of life. As always, Ford searches for images that have an independent effect requiring no explanations. In this film he wanted to interject what he had left out when he previously rendered woman as the protector of the species. He does not seek the homogenous presence of woman, but rather femininity in all its forms: In the face of risk, in her religious function, subordinated to the maternal and sexual instinct. Briefly, perhaps even Lesbos makes an appearance among them. As it is not a pleasant story, the film is a work of art that develops around femininity and sex without the usual tribute that erotic films tend to give to beauty. In spite of the connection we strive to make between both concepts, sexual attraction has little to do with beauty. It is spontaneous, does not strictly follow the aesthetic norms and is the result of uncontrollable impulses that go beyond the concept of the perfect line. Proportions and symmetry are the essence of the definition of beauty. Nonetheless, among the exciting images assaulting our brains it is precisely the asymmetrical and disproportional that awakens our desire with irrational force. While exaggerated forms contradict the proportions and limits of the line demanded by beauty, excessive curves in a woman can cause a sexual stimulus in a man. Only art can reconcile the display of beauty with sex in its purest conception. Within the renowned sculptural form of "Venus de Milo," beats an exuberantly sensual force unrelated to beauty that resides in the disproportion of its forms, the opulent hips that offer fertility, and the uneven gesture of the figure. A perfectly proportioned and static sculpture would undoubtedly be admired by our eyes, but would fail to excite the rest of our senses. Beauty produces a seductive and soothing sensation that invites reflection. At the other—much less rational—end of the subconscious, the sexual message is like a mysterious narcotic that is disturbing and drives us to action. Because sex does not adjust its activity to the norms of beauty, music—the least formal of the arts—is the one most frequently present during amorous ecstasy. In cinema the sexual relationship of the hero and heroine in the movie is almost always between actors and actresses whose appearance in some way adjusts to the classical standard of beauty or who can at least pretend to adapt to it. When it is a matter of suggesting the existence of erotic relations between individuals less physically attractive or of a repellent appearance, it is generally with the purpose of indicating the inferior moral condition of the participants or to emphasize the degrading actions of one of the two protagonists. This theatrical representation seeks a particular relationship between eroticism and aesthetics in relation to morals but does not reflect the true nature of sex. It is simply a classical idealization: The balance that ancient Greece searched for within human passions with respect to ethical thought, beauty, and art.

The ingredients of beauty are not really conditioned to the sexual instinct. Sometimes we observe them working against each other; it seems as if these sensations affect two different portions of our brains. In the classical era, art was able to unite them, but sex and beauty are usually antagonistic. Nonetheless, they do have something in common—both can be affected by context. To use a somewhat cinematographic example: The voluptuousness of Sofia Loren's body, capable of exciting uncontrollable masculine sexual impulses, would develop into revulsion if those same succulent breasts were transposed upon the virile image of John Wayne, becoming ridiculous protrusions that would give his figure a truly grotesque appearance. In this case the alterations mentioned have almost the same effect on beauty as they do with respect to sex, but this coincidence doesn't happen very often. Without a doubt the aesthetic perception and the sexual reaction obey different drives that generally remain disassociated. The stimulus that drives sex definitely remains indifferent to the perfection of lines and does not conform to the satisfactions promised by beauty. When Stendhal stated that beauty was "a promise of happiness," he was undoubtedly referring to the concept of beauty within art. As far as sex is concerned, beauty promises nothing. Something like that can only be found in the lavish voluptuousness, feminine intelligence, and other aphrodisiacal attributes of women. Those almost-perfect female figures only satisfy fashion designers, hairdressers, and those interested in being seen in their company, without sex ever becoming a prominent protagonist. In the case of Cartwright, beauty resides in the heroic gesture of sacrifice that she makes, and at the same time, the sexual act is sublimated through the saving surrender of her femininity. Even though on this occasion they coincided, there is no doubt that within humanity, sex and beauty maintain an unstable relationship. To compose his story, in *Seven Women* the artist has relied on the conflict provoked by a situation in which both beauty and the vile are present. Art is not a synonym of beauty. It doesn't even have to be associated with it, as most people believe.

A precise definition of art has eluded those who have attempted to make one, perhaps because art, just like sunlight or a perfume, passes through our senses before reaching our reason, and it is impossible to characterize these experiences. With the sensations that affect the subconscious we can only attempt descriptive comparisons, we are not able to define them. Through the excitement that it produces, we can recognize the existence of the work of art and, even while it is difficult for us to detail its contents, we might be able to value its components. The first thing that comes to our imagination is beauty, which as we have seen does not have a fixed meaning. For a mystic it could be represented by the gates that allow entry to paradise, but to an ethical enthusiast it might be reflected in a gesture of generosity and sacrifice. On the other hand, it is possible that the eye of the aesthete might only see within beauty the path that leads to perfection. Following this path, through sculpture beauty is idealized in Apollo, even though he is also associated with music and poetry within classic mythology. Something else is also related to art that apparently has been forgotten: More than anything beauty is also authenticity. So art can be accompanied by beauty or it can dispense with it. Beauty is not an indispensable element of art's content, nor does it define art. It is much easier to establish what art isn't. For example, decoration, reproduction, or good taste is not art. At the other end of the panorama, art is originality. To hurl imagination towards an unknown destiny is like science: A perpetual search without knowing what will be found. The most substantial distinction that can be made between someone who decorates or copies and someone who takes influences from the past to enhance their own inspiration is that this work will contribute and project towards the future, while the imitation is parasitic and only looks to the past. An artist has the sensibility that is open to everything that happens. One cannot be a poet by traveling the open road without removing a single rock or attempting to plant one flower.

During its premiere, *Seven Women* did not obtain the success this great film deserves. The public did not support it with its attendance, and it also did not receive a positive response from the critics at the time. Its failure is perhaps due to the expectation of yet another spectacular adventure movie like many productions of that era, this time located in the middle of Asia. Also, it was not the most appropriate time to develop a subject so removed from the most currently exciting political event. The American public was obsessed with the threat of the new regime. In 1966 the Cold War was at its peak and it would have been the ideal moment to make–using the same elements–another anticommunist campaign that would have surely been much better received. By updating the dates and renaming Tunga Commissioner everything would have been resolved; everything but the vital aura that must accompany any work of art, as this would have been struck down by the imposture. The explanation of the film's commercial failure is found in the superficial reaction of the masses to the silver screen and the public's frivolous disposition with respect to art in general. The audiences' feelings towards assorted creative expressions changes moment to moment, and the same representation can have a different meaning to a large audience of a different cultural level. The public attending certain artistic events is usually small and could be evaluated almost individually. The exhibitions of painting and sculpture, for example, are frequented by a limited number of attendees and are intended for a small group of connoisseurs and patrons who support the activities of museums, artists, and galleries. The rest of the turnout is frequently made up of individuals who, lacking a hobby, conceal their ignorance in the undefined world of aesthetics. Not having found a specific activity, these idle persons are distracted by what serves no particular function and has a subjective condition. A portion of the public that frequents events relating to art simulates a superficial interest in what they are seeing, and their attendance generally has the ingenuous purpose of giving themselves a more sophisticated appearance. During these events, certain snobs who wouldn't be able to identify an entire continent on a map entertain themselves with esoteric explanations that are outside anyone's reach. Fortunately, cinematography does not depend upon such a diminished public and, consequently, it is also not subjected to the individual influence of these impostors. However, it does have other problems: In cinema the masses impose their preferences without any consideration to the quality of the product. In either circumstance, the value of the work is only recognized by a minority, and the quality depends exclusively on the talent and determination of the artist. Those in favor of excellence are not sufficiently plentiful to impose their criteria on any of the art disciplines. As for the cinematography industry, the situation has not improved much over time. Today it is bankers who perhaps have the most influence on the ingredients that comprise a film. Productions on certain occasions require the investment of astronomical amounts of money that only a bank could finance, and the creators of a movie must subject their will to those who consider the search for quality a secondary objective. There are directors who have become famous billionaires by producing movies destined for virtually mentally handicapped viewers, while creators of truly valuable recent films such as Oliver Hirschbiegel's *The Downfall*," Alexander Payne's *Sideways*, Josh Sternfeld's *Winter Solstice*, and Todd Field's *In The Bedroom* remain unfamiliar to the public. Like other masterpieces, *Seven Women* will have to wait for recognition from future generations.

We cannot define it, we can't even describe it, we are only capable of feeling the sensation of its existence. And yet it is possible that art, as we currently conceive it, might have completed its cycle. Nobody can be sure da Vinci or Michelangelo, if alive today, would dedicate their talents and energies to the same activity that more than five hundred years earlier captivated their imagination. Even so, art continues to be creative: All that has changed are the methods of expression. Science has transformed our surroundings and altered our perception of the universe, it has expanded the expectations of the human being. And cinema is one of its consequences. Within film, accessories and unnecessary ornaments have very little to do with talent. In all artistic expressions, any excess elements are detrimental to the work; the magnificence of the scenes and the profusion of explanations impede the intimate encounter between the public and the representation being made. Ford's cinema rejects the superfluous and depends upon penetrating images that leave an intimate sensation in the mind of the viewer. Anyone with sensibility will discover something new and stimulating in each of his movies. With a minimum of dialogue, in *Seven Women* the director realizes a feat of profound communication among the characters. This film is one of his masterworks and, from a thoughtful point of view, is perhaps his best movie. To the end, John

Ford managed to remain at the height of his brilliance. He is one of the few artists who managed to create an authentic, comprehensible, and orderly body of work in the midst of the aesthetic chaos experienced by Western civilization during the past century. For some, living is the only way to declare themselves and their sole creative possibility; others have the ability to make an art out of life. With *Seven Women* we contemplate the brilliance of the sun sinking in the horizon, the final gesture of a giant who, with profound reverence for women, announces his departure.

The End

J.M. Tasende